MW01199138

Romancing the Trail:

Six Days Atop Laurel Ridge

Christine,

May every path you take
lead you to holy places.

DANE CRAMER

Romancing the Trail: Six Days Atop Laurel Ridge

Second Printing

Cover redesign by TG Graphics & Website Design: www.ttgray.com

ISBN: 978-0-9904474-3-6

PRINTED IN THE UNITED STATES OF AMERICA

To my parents (Ed & Margaret) –
who first taught me words.

The author would like to thank
Donna Pletcher & Sam Bowers of Laurel Ridge State Park,
Levi Foust,
Sherrie Pensiero for her encouragement and professional insights,
his daughter, Hannah, for the inside cover drawing,
and special thanks to his wife, Cynthia, for her love and support.

Edited by Sherrie Pensiero – The Write Solution
Somerset, PA
Front cover photo taken by Tim Segina, during his 2006
thru-hike with Richard Sabol, Jr. Used with permission.

PROLOGUE

It was a cold, relentless rain - the kind that saturated not only the clothing, but seeped even into the forgotten recesses of the soul. It could make the strong-willed repent, or bring forgiveness to the broken.

I tramped forward in the springtime deluge with head lowered to shield my face from the cold, wet wind. My feet danced unemotionally to the music of the rain. I jumped across the trail and skipped over a deep puddle. After sidestepping a slippery rock, I paused to look back. Not far behind me trekked Week Knees. He leaned his frame into the same wind and walked with his eyes to the trail, keeping a vigilant lookout for water-saturated earth that needed only a slight push to take a leg where it ought not to go.

We were not far from our objective. My backpack felt like a dragging anchor, weighed too far from shore. I had already begun imagining the relief I would experience as I would soon lower it. Yet, in spite of the desire to relieve myself of this persistent weight and find shelter from the rain, I felt a familiar twinge of melancholy. This happened whenever I neared the end of a hike, regardless of how unkind the trail had been, or cold the wind had blown.

I stopped to catch my breath and turn away from the cruel rain. Looking back the trail I waited for Week Knees, when suddenly, like the morning sun over an eastern sky, a peculiar thought rose up within me. I toyed with it for only a moment, and then resolved – there in the cataclysm of rain – to return to this trail, walk it in its entirety, and translate that struggle to writing.

Week Knees reached my side, and as he stopped in the beating rain, I shared with him my thought. Reaching inside of his jacket he retrieved his smoking pipe and filled it with sweet-smelling tobacco from a foiled pouch. Lighting the dark powdery leaves, he let the smoke filter its way upward through the drenched air while I watched. He did not say, but I believe that he liked the idea.

Day One

If the content of our days could be so divided, then during the course of each twenty-four hour cycle it is probably safe to say that each one of us makes hundreds of trips. Just after our eyes begin to flicker in the morning light, we begin a series of trips that will last the daylong. Perhaps we start with a trip from our beds to the bathroom. From there we might make a trip to the kitchen where we fumble sleepy-eyed over the coffeepot. After another trip back to our bedroom, one to the kitchen, and once more to the bathroom, we may then make a trip to the driveway to begin yet another trip. That one may take us to our place of employment, our school, or wherever it is that we spend the bulk of our day.

We continue to travel from here to there; to fetch this or deposit that; to meet someone or avoid another; to earn; to spend; to profit someone or to serve ourselves. Though we sometimes regret having to make some trips – without them our lives would not only be incomplete – but, I dare say, we would soon perish in their absence. And at the close of the day when we feel that we can finally cease from our activities, we are in reality only resting between trips. If indeed we rest at all, for it is then that our minds really seem to begin their own wanderings.

As a truth, if it were not for the wonderful trips conducted by our minds, our days would not be so tolerable. I fear that it would be nearly impossible to count the number of times during the course of the day that our minds have transported us to places that our bodies longed for but could not for the moment enjoy. Sometimes we take these cerebral trips to find adventure, while at other times we simply need a way to escape the common drudgeries of life.

Each trip that we make, if left alone, remains just a trip. However, if we see our trips not as individual ventures but as a part of something larger, then we no longer are merely making a trip – we are on a journey. And if on the journey we pause to savor our travel, meet those around us and listen to the sound of our own footfalls, then our trip has become an odyssey.

Months had passed since that springtime hike in the pouring rain with Week Knees when the thought of an emblazoned hike in the form of a book birthed into my mind. Though life's busyness drew me back into its spinning cyclone, I did not forget my rain-borne desire. As time passed my resolve to return to the trail strengthened until finally the day came upon me that I could begin my forest odyssey.

On my living room floor I knelt in the midst of the mounds of camping items and food supplies that were set in a circle about me. Packing for a trip is no less important than the trip itself. Setting a tent up in the dark and rain is not the time to remember that the tent poles are still stowed in the garage. Digging in your sack for an extra sweater as the temperature drops is not the time to discover that it was left behind. So, not wanting to miss a thing, I carefully subdivided my camping goods into gear and clothing sections, and then stacked my food provisions into breakfast, lunch, dinner and snack piles. Working against a checklist, I made certain that I was not forgetting any necessities.

While looking over the collection of goods, I noticed that nothing, in itself, seemed too heavy. But that sense, I have learned, can be deceptive. When the sum total of many light items are lifted in a pack, and placed like a yoke over the shoulders, it is an alarming surprise to discover just how quickly they have added themselves together.

Backpacking is a curious beast. A backpacker may hike, but a hiker is not necessarily backpacking. A backpacker will camp, but a camper is not, by virtue of camping, backpacking. To backpack, the journeyman carries in a pack, which is usually fastened over the shoulders and slung onto the back, every essential item needed for the trip. The kitchen, pantry, and bedroom are all carried somewhere in the bowels of the backpack. Food, shelter, and water must be taken into consideration first, and most every other item then orbits around these basics.

Naturally, weight becomes a premium consideration since all of these items must be carried wherever the backpacker goes. With the compliments of a hot sun and several steep hills, a seemingly light backpack at the beginning of a trip can feel as though it contains a blacksmith's anvil by the end of the day.

Helpful items are sometimes discarded based merely on their weightiness. Shopkeepers who sell backpacking equipment know to keep a small scale in their store so they can answer that oft-asked question, "how much does it weigh?" I must confess that I have even purchased a number of items, not because they were invaluable to me on the trail, but because they simply did not weigh much.

Take, for instance, my combination thermometer/whistle. I've never had anyone race up to me in the woods, and with desperation in their voice, beg for the current temperature.

Nor have I ever been trapped in a threatening situation, which daring escape could only come by persistent and clever whistling. But at only a few ounces, the gimcrack was a must-have, and I felt it looked quite handsome clipped to my shoulder strap.

So, my thermometer/whistle would go on this trip, but my GPS would stay behind – it was too heavy, and there would be no need for global positioning via satellite on the well-marked footpath that I intended to suffer.

Piece-by-piece, I sorted through the items, setting aside those things that I could not, or would not take, while placing inside my backpack that which I felt would be necessary or useful. My pack steadily grew both in bulk and weight, until I felt quite satisfied that I had all that I needed to survive the seventy miles of earthen highway, which stretches across the ridge of Laurel Hill.

Pennsylvania has three mountain ranges, the Appalachian, the Pocono, and the Allegheny, which are all part of the larger Appalachian System. Within the Allegheny Mountain Range, there are two distinct ridges that appear on a topographical map, as smaller, straying ripples, running parallel with each other: Chestnut Ridge to the west and Laurel Hill to the east. Both hills have stood as significant and stubborn obstacles for the settlers moving west during the early, expansive period of our country. Dr. Joseph Schoepf, while traveling from Bedford, Pennsylvania, to the area known today as Pittsburgh, Pennsylvania, in 1783, described the ruggedness of Laurel Hill in *A Hiker's Guide to the Laurel Highlands Trail*:

> *... A desolate and wild mountain it is, its ridge and western slope exhausting horse and man; not so much because of steepness, as on account of the abominable rock fragments*

lying in the greatest confusion one over another and over which the road proceeds.

Laurel Hill forms the western boundary of the Pennsylvanian County in which I have always called home – Somerset. Laurel Hill stretches northeastward from the banks of the frothy whitewaters of the Youghiogheny River coursing through Ohiopyle, Pennsylvania, to the deep Conemaugh Gorge, whose cutting crevice slices into the northwestern edges of Johnstown, Pennsylvania.

Growing up in Lincoln Township, my early life was formed within easy sight of Laurel Hill. There I saw it seaming together the wondrous blue skies that canopied my youth, and the fertile Pennsylvania soil that continually rose in ancient friendship to meet it. Across the ridge of this mountain range meanders the Laurel Highlands Hiking Trail. It is a seventy-mile scenic pathway traversing State Park soil, Pennsylvania Game Lands, State Forests, and private property. It attracts thousands of hikers, hunters, campers, and backpackers every year, who each attend for their own sacred purposes.

When I was a young boy, I often looked at the blue-tinted range, which seemed so far away, and found myself swept up in imagination over the secrets that were surely hidden in its hills and hollows. Therefore, having felt its lure for a considerably long time, I was quite content with the plan to spend the next six days stepping over its rocks, sleeping in its gullies, and wandering beneath its rich, leafy coverings.

I had hiked every section of this trail at least once, but had never made an end-to-end trek. In backpacking vernacular, walking from end to end on a trail is referred to as a "thru-hike." For a long time I had considered a thru-hike. Mostly, the inspiration came as I was driving over the Laurel Ridge. Watching the forest roll past my open window, I would swear that I could hear my name being whispered by the grand mountain. But it was not until then, in that springtime rain, that I decided it must be done.

Finally, an aperture in my schedule appeared, and I jumped at the opportunity. Ardent plans to make this extended walk were quickly made, and I notified my three hiking companions. These men introduced me to backpacking over a decade ago on the Laurel Highlands Hiking Trail, and let me tag along with them through the woods.

I can vividly recall the first time I ever attended one of their walks. I had over-filled a borrowed backpack, and walked in canvas tennis shoes. I carried a large, bright red sleeping bag that stuck so far out of my pack that I had to literally turn sideways to walk through some sections of the trail. Nervously, I approached the woods, fearful that I would fail the forest's stringent examination. But, that first autumn walk was kind to me, and the woods drew me back again and again. My friends continued to lead me, and I followed where they walked, taking the trails they sought.

In time I cut myself loose from this apprenticeship of sorts, and began to seek out other paths, which would lead me by quiet glens, marshy meadows, scattered rocks, and rolling hills. Those places were also generous to me, and I continued replenishing my backpack for new adventures. However, regardless of where I roamed, I often returned to the familiar woods of the Laurel Highlands Hiking Trail.

When it became certain that I could make this walk, I sent notice of my intentions to my hiking comrades, known in my hiking journals by their trail names: Week Knees, Dream Weaver, and Moocher, and invited them to come along for this mid-summer walk.

Now, I do not know how or when trail names first appeared. But I first learned about them while hiking sections of the Appalachian Trail. There, hikers were using these creative monikers to identify themselves to other hikers. It became their identity while living on the trail. Sometimes the people who walked closest to a hiker never even knew his or her given name – only their trail identity. I have never heard an explanation of a name that did not have an interesting story behind it, or some meaning attached to it. Some are clever, some are funny, and all seem to carry something of the person's heart.

One name that made me smile was discovered while I was reading a shelter register, which was signed by an Appalachian Trail thru-hiker named, *Never Again*. Then, there was *Buckeye*, who hailed from Ohio, and a southbound thru-hiker who called himself, *South Wind*. My companions and I met *Beetle* in Connecticut, who was collecting insect samples for her boyfriend, and *Einstein's Human* who claimed that his dog, Einstein, named him. In Massachusetts, we met a slow, but steady moving senior citizen named *La-Tortuga*. And one of my favorite's was a man we met in Pennsylvania who said that he began with the trail name, *Nomad*, but soon discovered there were so many Nomads hiking the trail, that he just started calling himself, *Ralph*.

When I began my first hiking journal, I asked each of my friends to come up with a suitable trail name. I believed that my journals would glow with a little more magic if everyone adorned an enduring, rough-and-tumble trail identity. It also seemed like a good way to protect our families in the event of a feckless casualty, or woodsy misdemeanor.

If memory serves me correctly, David Jack, one of my hiking gurus, had been napping beside a Connecticut brook when the inspiration for the trail name *Dream Weaver* came upon him. David Trent, another one of my hiking masters, was not so impromptus. While still pondering a number of possibilities, he was on the trail once and was adjusting his knee wrap when he announced that he had only a week's worth of walk in his knees – the name stuck, and *Week Knees* was born.

Terry Maurer had been notoriously known to us as someone who was forever forgetting something on a trip. We always argued that his pack was lighter than ours because we were carrying the things he would later need. Therefore, we agreed with his choice of a trail name – *Moocher*.

The name that I have hiked with for years, and have scribbled across countless hiking registers along many trails, sprang out of a certain affinity that I have for flight and history, and for an appreciation of very strong people I have known. Watching old newsreels of B-17s and B-24s returning home from battle over European and Pacific theaters during World War II, I became enthralled with their durability. Taking on significant battle damage, these great airplanes lumbered home often by turning a propeller into the wind – feathering the prop – when the engine was dead. Limping back as they did, their crews often were able to live to fly again.

This reminded me how we who walk the earth can be like those old airplanes that once dotted the skies. We endure strife and take on battle damage. We undergo attacks and carry in our body wounds, and in our hearts scars that tell tales of sometimes very vicious wars. Yet, as a testament to the Engineer who designed us, we not only fly again, but are often given to soaring. I have met many people who have 'feathered a prop' and kept on flying. Therefore, the name *Featheredprop* seemed an excellent way for me to mark my fascination of flight, and to honor those I know who persistently fly aloft with sputtering engine or damaged wingtip.

As I prepared for this trip I asked my friends to once more don their alter egos and join me on my summer hike upon the Laurel Highlands Hiking Trail. I gave them my hiking itinerary and left them to decide if they would join me. But whether they accepted my invitation or not, my intent would be unhindered. Alone, or in the company of others, I had endeavored to walk for the next few days.

As I got up from my living room floor, and grunted slightly beneath the weight of my forty-two-pound pack, I was feeling an excitement to finally make this walk. I laced my boots, slipped on my cap, and did a hindmost look about my place. Satisfied that I had everything that I needed, I began my odyssey.

Today's walk would not be a long one, and so I did not get started until the afternoon hours. I drove with my Uncle George in the seat beside me, to neighboring Fayette County, where I would begin my journey.

Uncle George had agreed to return my vehicle to my parents who would pick me up in six days. While we traveled, I encouraged him to tell me again about his Army Air Force career. Buoyant with my questions, he reminisced of how he had hoped to learn to fly the agile P-38 Lightening fighter plane in World War II, but was instead assigned to pilot the B-29 bomber. He said that he was working to pass his final piloting tests when the war ended.

Since the Army no longer needed as many pilots, he told me that he chose to return to civilian life. I have several models of the strange looking Lockheed P-38 that tormented both German and Japanese pilots during the war, and am simply enchanted by its unique shape. It was exciting to think that my uncle beside me was somehow connected to both the Lockheed Lightening, and the powerful Boeing Superfortress that eventually brought that terrible war to a close.

We finally arrived in Ohiopyle, Pennsylvania, and turned down Garrett Street. The pavement of this short street soon gives way to gravel, and then to dirt before reaching its driveable end. From that point, it continues to narrow until it becomes a footpath, blending into the Laurel Highlands Hiking Trail. The trail can also be reached by descending a trail from the Trail Head Parking Lot, not far from where we were. However, joining the Laurel Highlands Hiking Trail that way bypasses about the first one-half mile of the trail. That simply would not do. I wanted to begin my walk from the very roots of the dirt corridor, where the rocks and roots are pulled back from the terra firma to form the earliest appearance of a recognizable path. From there I hoped to walk it until from beneath my feet it had completely dissolved, and I could shake free from my boots the very last vestige of its fertile sod.

Ohiopyle is a bustling town – especially in the summer months. The town's centerpiece is the Ohiopyle Falls, where the Youghiogheny River plummets over the rocks between the south edge of town, and Ferncliff Peninsula. This natural gazingstock provides scenic backdrop to the boaters, kayakers, fishermen, and hikers who visit the river and the State Park Land surrounding the town. Though somewhat contested by the increased attention being paid to the fine regional biking trails, the river still attracts adventurers from all over the country who challenge the Class III & IV whitewater rapids of the "Lower Yough."

On numerous occasions I have had the opportunity to raft the raging Lower Yough. I have prided myself on the fact that I've never been in a boat that has capsized, nor have I been tossed into the river. However, despite this accomplishment, my rafting trips have not been unremarkable.

One particular excursion will always vividly stand out in my mind. I had invited some friends from work on an outing that included a rafting trip on the Lower Yough. Jenny, a woman whom I did not expect to accept the invitation, and her husband, Franklin, came along. He was retired, and she was a few years his junior. I was a little surprised when they showed up, and so I reminded them that this was *whitewater*. They shrugged off my warnings, and I did not feel that it was my place to question their gumption.

Jenny wore a clip-on sun visor that was loosely attached to her perfectly set hair, and Franklin had on a pair of slip-on loafers that closely resembled my father's bedroom slippers. I tried to encourage Jenny to at least buy a string from one of the local outfitters to secure her prescription eyeglasses, but she laughed at my over-cautious attitude. I could not shake this foreboding feeling that they were both fraught with the illusion of a lazy afternoon canoe trip down a sleepy river. In any event, we climbed aboard a large rubber raft and pushed off.

As we approached the first rapid I glanced behind me and saw Jenny smiling broadly, dipping her paddle into the frothing waters with Franklin beside her engaged in a one-sided conversation about their good fortune of being on the river on such a sunny day.

The first rapid we encountered was a relatively mild, but long, introductory rapid known as Entrance Rapid. We had just begun our navigation of the rapid when we heard a splash that sounded unusually loud. I turned around to find Jenny's seat oddly vacant. Her sun visor was beside the raft and speeding past us in the river. Jenny very quickly bobbled to the water's surface beside the raft. Her eyeglasses were no longer on her nose and her smile had been replaced with a mixture of fear and anger that to this day has not been duplicated by anyone I know.

We threw our arms out to her and with no small amount of difficulty, drew her back into the relative safety of the raft. However, our rest was short-lived. As we struck the next rapid Franklin left the boat and we were soon busied with the task of retrieving him.

For the remaining series of rapids they seemed to politely take turns being thrown into the drink. I became rather adept at pulling them into the raft, and eventually learned that if you seize the overboard person by the life jacket, and fall backward into the boat, you can more easily heave the rafter-turned-swimmer over the sides, and into the innards of the raft. The rest of our party – those who were safely tucked away in another raft – shouted constant encouragement, and tried to assure us that they, too, were having their fair share of troubles. Their troubles, however, seemed limited to the difficulty of navigating around the contents of our raft frequently set afloat.

When we were not retrieving bodies from the water, or lying exhausted on the bottom of the raft, we seemed to be continually getting hung up on the many rocks that jaggedly protruded from the river's surface.

On one particular rock, the starboard side of the raft became pinned, lifting the raft to a near vertical position. Taking our oars so that they would not become swept away by the swirling river, we all climbed out upon the rock. We tried in vain to dislodge the raft but the intense hydraulic pressure kept it securely against the rock.

"I think I can free it," Franklin said with an air of confidence that fooled no one.

He slid off the rock and into the raft. With both legs

knee-deep in the raging water he stood on the port side of the raft and began to jump up and down, trying to wrestle the boat free from the grip of the river. Those of us who did not want to spend the rest of the day on the small rock tried to encourage him.

"That's it, Franklin, I think I saw it move," I lied.

"Come on, honey," Jenny shouted, "I think you almost have it."

"Try jumping over here, Franklin," I directed, "we'll be off this rock in no time."

Suddenly, Franklin stopped. Slowly he lifted his head and looked at each of us. There was a pained expression on his face. He was quiet for a moment, and it seemed as though he was trying to figure out how to share something very difficult with us.

Finally, he spoke. "I've lost my shoe."

Pulling his left leg out of the water he revealed a stockinged foot minus the slip-on shoe. The hydraulic pressure of the river had washed it off of his foot. Franklin really seemed to be taking the loss hard.

"That was a good shoe," he said with bowed head.

"I'm sure that it was Franklin, but we really must try to get off of this rock," I said, trying to redirect his focus.

"Do you think we'll be able to find it?" he asked innocently.

I looked around at the raging rapid that we were in the center of. The water was foaming white as it churned and splashed past us at a terrific pace. The possibilities of finding his shoe somewhere out on this wild river seemed minuscule.

"Oh, I'm sure it will show up. We'll be sure to check with the Lost and Found Department before we leave," I said, trying again to redirect his attention. I hoped that he did not realize that the river did not have a Lost and Found

Department.

Franklin seemed encouraged with the thought and was soon back to shaking the boat. How he did it I am not certain but suddenly the boat became righted and slid free from the rock. There was a look of triumph on his face that suggested to me we were witnessing his finest hour. However, his victory was short-lived. For, he realized that he was alone in the boat and we had all of the oars. His victorious countenance became replaced with the fear that we had grown accustomed to all morning.

We had no choice but to seize the oars and leap into the rapids to try and catch Franklin. I recall thinking, as I hit the cold water and began swimming through the rapid, that this day may well go on forever.

Finally we caught Franklin and climbed aboard the raft. Not far down the river, Franklin suddenly called out "Look, a shoe!"

We paddled in the direction of his wild gesturing and held the boat still in the current as Franklin fished an old tennis shoe out of the water. Apparently its previous tenant had an adventure similar to Franklin's. Much to everyone's surprise, it fit his left foot. He tied it tightly and we pushed off.

After our adventure-laden trip was over, and we were waiting for a return ride to Ohiopyle, a young man, wearing only one shoe, recognized his tennis shoe on my shipmate's foot. Franklin was forced to surrender the shoe to its rightful owner, and limp back home.

The trip became a rather tender subject between Jenny and me, who injured her knee against a rock while challenging the last rapid from outside of our craft. After the incident, her knee always gave her advance warning of changing weather conditions, but Jenny took no solace in that. It was a few years before we could actually speak about it without me profusely uttering apologies for the misery that her injuries had induced.

One of the earliest whitewater rafters of the Youghiogheny River was a young and ambitious officer named George Washington. In May of 1754, the twenty-two year old Lieutenant Colonel was attempting to reach and dislodge the French from Fort Duquesne, located at the confluence of the Ohio, Monongahela and Allegheny Rivers, in what is now known as Pittsburgh, Pennsylvania. Building a road over Laurel Hill to the Ohio Fork was tedious work, and so the creative Washington sought an alternative passage via the Youghiogheny River.

All was going well for the aspiring military leader until he reached the dangerous Ohiopyle Falls, where he was forced to abandon his idea of a watery ride to the French-held fort. He returned to his camp at Fort Necessity, about nine miles away, and days later, on May 28, 1754, engaged the French in what became the opening battle of the French and Indian War at Jumonville Glen.

It is not clear who fired the first shot that day – the French, or Washington's troops, and it is unclear why shots were fired at all. The French insisted that they were on a peaceful envoy, but Washington declared evidence to the contrary. Whatever the case may be, he emerged victorious from the fifteen-minute skirmish, and took a number of French prisoners. The French commander, Ensign Joseph Coulon, Sieur de Jumonville, was killed in the clash. However, a single French-Canadian soldier, Monceau, who reportedly was in the woods answering nature's call at the time of the battle, escaped barefoot, and returned to the French post at Fort Duquesne.

When Commander Contrecoeur at Fort Duquesne learned of the battle, he dispatched a large regiment of French and Indian troops, led by Jumonville's brother,

Captain de Villers, on a punitive mission to meet Washington.

On July 3, 1754, the two forces met at Fort Necessity, not far from Ohiopyle, and an all-day battle ensued in a heavy rain. Washington was outgunned and was facing a dismal, short-lived future, when, surprisingly, the French offered him a truce. Washington wisely accepted and learned that day to never allow himself to be surrounded again. But, just as importantly, he lived to fight another day. He and his men marched out carrying full military colors, while the French burned Fort Necessity to the ground.

During a visit to Fort Necessity National Battlefield one day, I left the Park Office and strolled down to the meadows where the reconstructed palisade is located. Approaching the grassy lowland I saw an eerie sight that literally stopped me in my tracks. At the edge of the woods, just a short distance from the fort, stood an intimidating Native American warrior. He was Herb Clevenger, the Park's Native American Specialist. Dressed in the primitive garments of the regional Native American, he had his head shaved, but for a strip of hair down the middle and he held a war club folded across his arms.

As I saw him standing in his garb against the backdrop of the Pennsylvania forest, I had, for a fleeting moment that day, felt as though I was translated back to the days when the wooded pathways of Laurel Hill were not so friendly, and not so peaceful.

The grassy meadows of Fort Necessity National Battlefield, and the rocky ledges of nearby Jumonville Glen are both beautiful, quiet places. Of the meadow in which Fort Necessity was erected, Washington wrote that it was "a charming place for an encounter." It is charming indeed. Standing at both of these historical landmarks one can almost hear the musket volleys still reverberating as our country, and one of its emerging, youthful leaders, began their concerted birthing pangs.

I could faintly hear the roar of the Ohiopyle Falls as I thanked my uncle for his assistance, and watched him drive away in my van. I then turned my back on the town, and began my walk. The spectacular color of a pebble on the path caught my attention. I scooped it up, and placed it in my pocket for good luck.

My pack was heavy, but I enjoyed its snug feeling against my back. Walking towards the woods, I felt a smile creep across my face. I was finally going to begin my thru-hike, and I was excited about the venture.

As the path beneath my feet narrowed, and the trees moved closer to my side, I had the unmistakable awareness of having been conveyed from the confines of my familiar, comfortable world to one more rugged. This was chiefly made known to me through the distinct aroma of a living forest. If colors had redolence, then it was the fragrance of green that I perceived. My lungs were filled with the wooded-balm, and I was flooded with memories of many youthful walks, and playful jaunts that I had taken in my childhood days.

My Dad and his father had cut from a few acres of trees, a place for our family. Like sand around a sea, the woods encompassed our house with our back door swinging open just feet from the timber shoreline. Within moments of bursting free from our house, my siblings and I could be running through the woods, leaping over fallen logs, or twisting around trees, while rock-hopping our merry way to whatever adventure our insouciant minds might create. It was there, during those pleasurable excursions that I became familiar with the wondrously intoxicating, overwhelmingly pleasant smell of green.

Moving to the beginning of the Laurel Highlands Hiking Trail, I saw the first of many yellow blazes that would accompany me during my journey. Each blaze is a painted 2" x 5" stripe appearing on trees or rocks approximately every 100 feet along the trail. At a few places, because of the varying terrain, the trail can become indiscernible. It is at those junctures that the blazes are most important.

Walking more than five minutes without seeing a blaze is a good sign of being lost. Even experienced hikers will wander off the trail at times. I once met a backpacker on the Appalachian Trail in Connecticut who had been on the trail for months. He confessed that there was hardly a day that went by that he did not accidentally stray from the path.

Almost immediately the Laurel Highlands Hiking Trail turned steeply upwards as the woods closed even more securely about me. The Youghiogheny River parallels the trail to the southeast, sandwiching in the old B & O Railroad tracks. The railroad first came to Ohiopyle (known then as Falls City) in March of 1871. The train tracks soon brought vacationers from Pittsburgh to Falls City and back home for one dollar. The influx of tourists created the need for hotels. Four were raised in-town, and in 1879, on Ferncliff Peninsula, a stately, four-story hotel was built.

But these resort accommodations lasted only until the traveler's door to the world was flung more widely open by the introduction of the automobile. Soon, the hotels, boardwalks, and ball fields on Ferncliff Peninsula were removed. The forest replenished itself and it is now a delightful place to hike. From the labyrinth of walking trails on the peninsula, there are numerous vantage points where one can watch the swiftly moving Youghiogheny churn by.

As I walked the Laurel Highlands Hiking Trail, I could hear hollering from the river beside me. Looking through the thickly-leafed trees, I could see people sitting in rafts, drifting down the river. From the bellies of these rubber crafts came their jovial shouts. They were rafting the more mild section of the river, above the Ohiopyle Falls, and would soon be making their exit. This section is known as the Middle Yough. I rafted it once on a rubber raft, and found it to be a slow-moving, enjoyable trip, with very little whitewater.

Down the river from this point, ropes with buoys stretch across the water to keep swimmers and boaters safely away from the falls. On Ferncliff Peninsula there are several lifesaver rings attached to ropes, and secured to posts, positioned as silent sentinels near the falls. Should someone move past the buoys and ropes, these rings could be tossed out into the water, becoming a person's last hope before passing over the falls.

Moving northward on the trail, I soon came upon the first milepost. The Laurel Highlands Hiking Trail, which is entirely managed by the Pennsylvania State Park Commission, is conveniently measured by markers posted every mile along the trail. They are concrete pillars, standing about two-feet tall. The one I stood before was marked with a "1." My quest was to find sixty-nine more just like it. But, that would take some more walking. I took a deep, determined breath and, enjoying the way it sounded, stepped past the pillar.

The Youghiogheny River provided initial companionship as I walked northward. But as the trail continued to ascend, the river went on her own way, leaving me only with its diminishing rushing chorus. My breathing became noticeably labored as I scaled the 750-foot ascent occurring over the first mile. The trail leveled off slightly, and then continued to climb until it reached a popular vista overlooking what is known as Victoria Flats. From here, the Youghiogheny River can be seen making a sharp bend to the northwest, as it flows toward Ohiopyle.

Victoria had once been a small town, stationed inside of the horseshoe bend of the river. Now, few maps even record the mark it once held in the world. Prior to 1800, settlers discovered a salt spring on the flatland near the Youghiogheny, which was attracting the animals as a salt lick. Small quantities of salt were boiled free from the water and used by the local people. From 1812 to 1819, a man named Thomas Meason operated a salt-works from the meadows, but gave it up when the enterprise became unprofitable.

The railroad tracks were eventually constructed over the old salt works furnace, effectively obliterating any suggestion of it. But, settlers continued to live in the region, and drew their salt from the spring. A railroad siding was eventually established, and Victoria's Post Office began operations in 1892. The late historian, J. Meyers, recorded that the town was named after Victoria Balsey, but he left his readers with no information as to who she was, or what impact she may have had on the small community.

Weeks after my hike, I returned to the area and made an attempt to access Victoria Flats. However, Rock Spring Road, which leads to Victoria, soon runs out of pavement, and did not seem welcoming to the low-clearance of my mini-van. Turning around, I made my way out, but decided to stop and talk with a neighboring gentleman who was working in his backyard.

He was friendly, and as I began to ask more detailed questions of the area, he directed me to his father, John Williams, Jr., who lives nearby. Mr. Williams was not at home, but I was able to reach him later by phone. He quickly volunteered to shuttle me down the road in his four-wheel drive truck – an offer I simply could not turn down. So, weeks after my hike, on a rainy Saturday morning, I pulled into the Williams' driveway, excited to view the flats from the ground floor.

Climbing out of my van, I first met Mrs. Fay Williams, who was dog-sitting that day at their blue-painted block house. She told me that the local campground does not permit unsupervised dogs to be left at the campground, and so they direct the dog owners to her place. The owners of the two dogs she was watching that day were spending the day on the river. She seemed happy to have them, and the dogs seemed quite content to be under her conscientious care.

Mr. Williams was in his shop when I arrived, but directly made his way to the driveway. I shook his hand and introduced myself. He offered a smile that I saw frequently that day, and told me that everyone just calls him "Junior." On the south side of seventy years, Junior did not look his age. Thin, with strong arms, he runs a small farm, and enjoys woodworking in his impressively equipped shop. For nearly thirty years, he drove daily from his home near Ohiopyle, to the mills in Homestead, Pennsylvania, where he worked as an equipment operator. He loves to timber, and was still cutting down trees for woodworking and to feed the fires in his shop and home. An active volunteer fireman, Junior was the President of the Ohiopyle Volunteer Fire Department.

We climbed aboard his Ford truck, and drove to Rock Spring Road. Turning down this township-maintained road, we quickly became enveloped by the lush forest, which was broken only by the clay-colored dirt division called a road. Junior said that he continues to hunt these woods for turkey and deer, and as we bounced along, told me that fishermen use the rocky artery to reach secluded spots along the Youghiogheny River. Passing a small truck parked along side of the road, Junior suggested that the driver might be in the woods looking for Ginseng root that grows in the area. Other than the occasional fisherman or hunter, he said the road is not often used.

As we descended deeper into the flats, Junior pointed to the now thickly-wooded sections of the forest, and described how homesteads once stood at those places – recalling the names of the people who lived there, and the way they cut out a living for themselves in these rough woods. Sawmillers and farmers mostly inhabited and worked the hills, he said. Rounding bends on this nearly forgotten road, Junior would sweep his hand to the right or left, and show me where fields of corn or oats once waved in the wind. It was almost too difficult to imagine.

All of these places are now covered by the thick, nearly impenetrable forest groves. Pointing to one flat section of the forest, Junior told me that a very fancy farmhouse, with a large front porch once stood there. Across the road from it, in another section of trees, he described where a large red barn had been built. These structures, like their inhabitants, are now long gone. Even the smallest of openings is now covered by high, unmanaged grass, while the forest continually closes in on it. Occasional deer paths cross the area, but the paths where feet once trod are not to be seen. Junior told me that when the State acquired the land, they bulldozed the remaining buildings, and buried them beneath the dirt on which they once stood. Nothing remains but the memory – and with ever-fewer people to remember it, Victoria's final hope of being recalled grows dimmer.

Further down the road, Junior pointed to an area near the railroad tracks where the famed salt spring is. He said the spring still bubbles water out of the ground, but not with much output. The water then trickles across the ground until it reaches the nearby Youghiogheny. It seems that salt water is not uncommon in the area. Junior told me that while drillers were drilling the several gas wells in the area, they would occasionally hit a salt water vein. One vein, he recalled, was an artesian well, spraying salt water out of the ground, effectively killing all the vegetation in the immediate vicinity.

Finally, where the road ends, we reached the flats. This is the interior of the horseshoe shaped curve of the Youghiogheny River, about three miles southeast of Ohiopyle. Junior pointed up to the mountainside, 728 feet above, where I had stood so many times on the trail, and looked down. It was a new, exciting experience to finally look up. While we stood in the meadow, a train rumbled by. Many years ago, the train would have stopped. Passengers might have boarded, or disembarked, and staples for living in these difficult hills would have been left behind.

Victoria Flat is quiet now, save the sound of songbirds, or the occasional passing freight train. The spring, which brought the homesteaders, still weeps from the earth, but there is none to gather its salty water, or to reduce it to the basic preservative that was once so necessary to live here in the wild. The rain drove Junior and me back to the shelter of his truck, and we soon made our bumpy way out of this old country.

In the summertime the overlook from the Laurel Highlands Hiking Trail above Victoria Flats can be a little obstructed with the heavy foliage, but in the spring and fall the view is spectacular. I have scaled the hill many times, in different seasons, and in different weather conditions, and have never left disappointed.

As I stood on top of the pinnacle this first day of my hike, I watched the river flow far beneath my feet, with the mute railroad tracks pacing beside it. Two canoes came down the river, and I watched the riders navigate their pointed crafts around the sharp bend as they paddled unhurriedly downstream. Behind the canoes, upstream from the bend, rocks protruding from the river left a visible streak of whitewater. From this lofty height these stripes of white across the river looked like permanent chevrons athwart the muscular arm of the river.

Probably one of the most rewarding experiences for a backpacker is to reach a summit with a view. Taking off my backpack, I leaned it against a tree, and sat down on a rock ledge to take it in. Inspiration comes easily in places like this, and I soon lost myself in contemplative thought. However, a bird, somewhere behind me in a thicket, brought me back with its singing. Without really thinking about it, I began tapping my foot in time to its chirping, counting the measure between its bursts.

When I realized what I was doing, I sat perplexed for a moment. This amazed me. How did this little creature come to know rhythm? I turned around to look for it, as if by seeing I would somehow know the answer to my question. But, I did not see the bird, and could only hear its singing.

I had probably heard something like this a thousand times, yet had never really thought about it. Rhythm. Out in the hinterlands, up on top of a savage summit where evidence of human influence is diminishing like the lowering sun, I found an untrained, undisciplined animal displaying an ordered recurrent meter. How could this be? Cadence works in accordance with time. Does this little bird have a concept of time? Does it know the difference between yesterday and today? Between this moment and the next? What does it know about the application of mathematical precision against the background of time to form rhythm?

These questions probed me. Yet, they also made me smile. For decades a great debate has raged among those who seek to understand the mysterious genesis of life. Some believe that the evidence around us points to life being intentionally caused by a Creator who, with intelligent design, made this world. Some believe that the same evidence suggests life was not the product of design, but came about as the result of natural reactions to random occurrences. Setting aside religious prejudices, I personally find it intellectually impossible to accept any theory suggesting that our very complex world is the result of chance happenings. Simply stated, there is just too much evidence of purpose to believe it came about by chance.

Take, for example, the bird singing behind me. Most likely it lives in a nest that it built. If we were to come across a nest in the woods, we would know instantly, because of its design, that something has built it. No one would assume that the wind, rain and sun built the nest through accidental force. That is because the nest, though very basic in design, is still too complex to cause anyone to believe that it could simply occur on its own. And where there is design, there must be purpose. And where there is purpose, there must be some form of intelligence. Forces like wind, rain, sunshine, gravity and inertia cannot create anything with a purpose, because they do not have a mind or will. Therefore, it seems clear to me that when we find something with design, we find purpose, and where there is purpose we can only assume that something more than a mindless force created it.

For years I have worked as an insurance claims investigator, and have investigated literally thousands of random occurrences for the purpose of determining the scope of someone's loss. In all of those events I have never found that the accidents improved upon property or body. Neither have I ever discovered that random occurrences brought about results with apparent design. For example, a tornado may knock down a grove of trees. But the trees do not fall in the shape of a house, or cut, split and stack themselves into firewood.

Intelligence, I have observed, is the only force that can effectively show design. If random occurrences were so effective in creating and improving, then surely we would employ it in our industry and medicine. For example, why does a doctor not prescribe a slip and fall for an aching back, and why do factories not use "accident lines" instead of assembly lines to make a product? If random occurrences brought about complex structures like our unfathomable brains, why do we not employ them to produce even simple designs? Why do we protect ourselves against accidents by buying insurance if accidents are so adept at bringing about positive changes? It is my belief that the working testimony of the world powerfully suggests that we simply do not believe random events can ever bring about the orderly, positive results, which only intelligence continues to produce.

I stared off the edge of the precipice, and considered not just the rhythmic bird, but also the complexities of the great ecological system of the forest, and the vast universe in which it is tucked – a universe that seems to bear strongly the thumbprint of structure, design, and purpose. It seems that order, precision, and rhythm, shower upon us, showing a design that cannot come but through an act of intelligent creation. Sing on little bird; sing on.

After an inspiring rest, I quit my wanderlust, and began hitching my backpack. As I was preparing to move north I heard voices ahead of me on the trail. The increased volume suggested that the sources of the voices were drawing nearer. I remained in the opening at the top of the hill so we could easily pass one another. Within a few moments two people emerged from the woods.

It took only a glance to see that the couple was a father and son team. The father appeared to be in his late thirties. The boy was probably nearing thirteen. They carried the same kind of backpack and walked with the same kind of shuffling movement.

"Howdy!" I called out as they stepped into the small opening.

"Hello there!" the father responded. They had apparently spotted me, as neither seemed startled.

"Beautiful day for a walk," I said.

"It sure is!" the eldest replied.

"Sure is!" his son echoed.

Noticing their heavy packs I asked, "Have you been on the trail very long?"

"This is our fourth day. We started at Route 271 and hiked the first day to Route 30. After that we hiked to Route 31, and yesterday we hiked to Route 653. We are putting in a long day today, and are finishing up at Ohiopyle."

"At Ohiopyle," the boy said as his dad finished speaking.

The two hikers were friendly but it seemed to me that neither might be really comfortable in social situations. They kept twisting, turning, and adjusting their packs while standing there. They also kept looking around as if hoping to find something more interesting than me.

"That's a pretty good trip," I said. They both glanced at me while I spoke and then began to look around again.

"Today's a real killer," the man said. "We knew it would be a long day but we didn't expect it to be this hard."

"To be this hard," his son said.

As we spoke about the weather and the condition of the trail, I noted that neither the father nor his son held any continual eye contact with me. They looked when they spoke, but then continued to look around as if the conversation lacked any real interest to them. And every time the man spoke, his son would glance up and help him finish the final thought.

"Have you seen anyone else out on the trail?" I asked.

"You gotta' guy who's ahead of you by about an hour. He's staying at the Ohiopyle shelters tonight and then moving north tomorrow," the man said.

"North tomorrow" came the echo.

"Yesterday we ran into a bunch of boys," the father continued. "I think they said they belonged to a club." He wrinkled his face, trying to squeeze something out of his memory. He then glanced at his son as if hoping for some help.

"Boy Scouts! I think that's who they were," the father said as the wrinkles left his face. He then glanced into the woods, responding to a noise that only he heard.

"Yeah, Boy Scouts," said the younger, evidently pleased because he thought he was helping.

"Two days ago," the father continued as he looked back my direction, "we ran into a woman out hiking by herself. She wasn't sleeping on the trail – just walking sections of it. 'Said that she was walking to clear her mind. I told her that I didn't think it was a good idea for her to be out walking alone. I'd never let my wife come out here to clear her mind alone."

"Not alone," reverberated the little fellow.

I wondered where the man's wife *did* go to clear her mind.

"Well," I said aloud, "I'd best be going."

"Alright then," the man said. "We ought to keep going ourselves. We're both anxious to get into town and get something to eat."

"Gotta get something to eat."

We turned from each other and started walking in different directions. I heard the two talking for a few moments before their voices faded from me.

One of my newest purchases was a hydration pack carried inside the top of my backpack. It is like an IV bag, with a connecting plastic hose clipped to my shoulder strap, near my mouth. At the end of the plastic hose is a bite valve. The bag is filled with water and whenever I want a drink I merely bite on the valve to release the flow of fluid into my waiting mouth. On a hot day like today, I kept up a pretty good flow. Thankfully, the path leveled off nicely, and I marched happily along, breathing prayers of thanksgiving for the strength and ability to be here.

Located about every eight to ten miles along the Laurel Highlands Hiking Trail is a shelter area. Each area consists of five "adirondack-styled," open-faced lean-tos, and about thirty tent sites. The lean-tos are numbered 1-5, and appear randomly scattered about the area. Before making an overnight trip on the Laurel Highlands Hiking Trail, the Park Commission requires reservations to be made. Donna Pletcher has been employed at the Park Office for over thirty-two years, and has worked out an interesting system for recording reservations.

She once invited me behind the counter and showed me a mammoth pegboard with columns divided by the eight shelter areas, and a month of days. Whenever she gets a call for a shelter reservation, she quickly looks at the pegboard from her desk and determines if there is a vacancy. When she takes a reservation, she places a peg into the board, showing that that particular lean-to is reserved. Because the system cannot record more than thirty-one days of reservations, no reservations can be accepted beyond that time frame.

The first night of this trip would be spent at the Ohiopyle Shelters – known to the Park staff as the Bidwell Shelters, named after the once-nearby town of Bidwell. Like Victoria, Bidwell is now a memory. When I later visited Victoria with Junior, we included a visit to Bidwell. This area is accessed by Bidwell Road, and is in even worse condition than the road leading to Victoria. Turning off of Maple Summit Road, Junior drove me down the twisting rocky road that descends for three miles into what he calls Cave Hollow. He said that Cave Hollow got its name from what was reported to be a very large cave that went deeply into the mountainside. He stopped his truck in front of some rock debris, and told me that this was once the entrance to the reported cave. He had never been inside, and in fact, cannot say for certain whether or not there was actually a cave there. But, when he was a young boy he had heard stories of how the old timers used to stop their horses at the cave, and take them inside to cool off as they were making their way out of the deep hollow.

One old timer, named Harry, was notorious for telling stories. Junior told me that one could only believe about one percent of what he said. He related that Harry used to tell how he once was ascending Bidwell Road, and stopped at the cave to take a break. When he walked in he said that he was nearly trampled by ninety-nine deer that came rushing out. When someone would challenge old Harry and ask how he knew it was not a hundred deer, Harry would respond, "Well, cursed-to-hell, I wouldn't tell no lie about one deer!"

Like Victoria, the area of Bidwell is now covered with forest, leaving no evidence to lead one to think that a small town once stood there. Near the bottom of the hill, Junior and I pulled off on a winding grass path, just wide enough to accommodate his truck. Following it to its end, Junior pointed into the trees and told me that an old cemetery lies just within. The rain was pouring in sheets, and so I threw on my raincoat, and ventured out into the woods, while Junior waited inside his truck. Using both hands to push my way through the thicket, I crawled through the woods until I stumbled over something.

Looking down I discovered that I had tripped over an old tombstone. There were no markings on it, and it was nearly sunk beneath the ground. Looking around I spied a few more grave markers, and slowly before my eyes, in the soaking rain, the Bidwell Cemetery began to materialize. Many of the markers that I saw were simply erected fieldstones. Junior told me that they were once engraved, but it is now apparent that their etched characters have eroded away. Some markers were shaped headstones, yet they too bore no telling of who slept beneath. One gravestone stood about three feet tall, and carried the name Morrison, with the date of death, 1881. Junior told me that several years ago someone had cleared the graveyard area, and the grass road leading to it. He estimated the vegetation that was now grown up around it to be about six or seven years old.

After leaving Bidwell Cemetery, Junior drove me to a flat area, near the Youghiogheny River. This, he told me, was where the Bidwell Train Station once stood. The area was partially cleared, and the tracks still wind by, but there is nothing to indicate that a railroad siding and telegraph station had been built there.

As I continued my thru-hike toward the shelters, I noticed that the sky was gradually changing. Rain clouds were mounting for a harsh display. Approaching the

Bidwell Shelter area, I saw campfire smoke drifting lazily upward to meet the dark clouds. Drawing closer, I saw a young man with his back to me, busying himself with the fire. A small nylon tent was pitched next to it. This was evidently the man that the father had told me about; and of whom the son had echoed.

He did not see me approach, and so I started shuffling my feet through the dirt to give him a gentle, subtle warning. He did not discern my faint bulletin, and so I called out a verbal salutation, "Hey there!"

The young man whipped quickly around and judging from the wide-eyed expression that he shot my way, it seemed that he had fancied himself alone in the woods.

"Hello!" He responded with the startled look still evident on his face as he stood up to meet me.

"I hope I didn't frighten you," I said, pretending not to notice his ashen appearance.

"Oh, not at all," he said with a crack in his voice.

"Nice fire you have there," I said, as I drew nearer.

The young man turned and studied the fire for a moment. Praising a fellow over his fire is like telling him that you like his pick-up truck, or row of antlers above the mantel of his fireplace. The feeling of pride can be irresistibly intoxicating.

He crouched down again and stirred the fire with a short stick that was resting against a nearby rock. This action sent a cloud of hot ash and smoke into the air, making the small fire look more impressive. He leaned back from the swirling smoke, and with the color now returned to his face, looked at me and said, "Yeah, thanks."

He was a thin man, probably in his early twenties. He wore denim jeans, a light blue T-shirt, ball cap and tennis shoes. He had thick eyeglasses on and looked more suited behind a computer desk than in the woods.

"How long are you out on the trail?" I asked.

"Well, this is my first night," he began, "I hiked in from Ohiopyle today, and am hoping to walk to the 653 Shelters tomorrow. The day after that I plan on hiking to the Route 31 Shelters before turning around and hiking the same route back to Ohiopyle." The young man stirred the fire again and sat back on a rock that edged the fire ring.

"Looks like I'll see you the next few nights then," I responded. "I'm staying at the same shelters for the next two nights but hope to keep going to the end of the trail."

"Awesome. I'd like to come back some time and do the whole thing too. Have you ever hiked this trail before?" he asked.

"I've never hiked it end-to-end, but I've done every section at least once. It's a great trail."

"The map shows a pretty steep hill just north of us. We'll probably hit it right away in the morning. Do you know anything about it?" he asked.

"Oh, you mean *Heart Attack Hill*," I replied. "Yeah, it's a tough one. It's very steep, and the climb never seems to end. But there's a nice view from the top. It'll be a good way to get you going in the morning," I laughed.

"Heart Attack Hill? Is it really that bad?" he asked with an eyebrow raised behind one of the thick lenses of his glasses.

"Oh, it's not too bad," I assured him. "Just take it slowly and rest as often as you need. It'll still be morning when we hit it so the temperature won't be too bad. When you reach the top there's a nice view on some rocks on the west side of the trail."

He started to ask me about the trail beyond the hill when a peal of thunder cracked violently above us.

"Wow, looks like we're in for a pretty good rain," I said. "I need to get going if I want to get some dry firewood before it begins."

"Okay, I'll talk to you later," he replied as he turned his attention again to the fire.

I walked over to Shelter No. 1, which I had reserved through the Park Office. As I put my pack down on the shelter floor the scattered raindrops that were now beginning to fall sounded out a tap-tap rhythm on the leaves above me. I noticed that whoever had last camped at the shelter left behind a nice little pile of firewood. I only needed to gather some kindling to get my blaze going.

Just as I returned with a load of small twigs, the sky opened up and a heavy rain began to fall. I watched my neighbor abandon his fire as he quickly gathered a few items and climbed into the safety of his tent.

All of the lean-tos have fireplaces constructed at the open-end side of the shelter. Although the chimneys do not exhaust well, the fires do a good job of taking the chill out of the shelter air on a cold night. When I had a nice fire going, I drew some water for dinner. The Park has wells drilled at each of the shelter areas and have installed hand pumps at ground level to draw the water. Along the Appalachian Trail, most water is drawn from springs or streams. So, to have a hand pump delivering water is considered a real luxury on the trail.

I fixed my dinner and coaxed the waning fire. After eating I stretched out on the wooden shelter floor atop my thin sleeping pad and relaxed. The rain continued to fall, and at times, came down in drenching sheets. Occasionally it blew through the shelter opening whenever the wind changed directions. I was glad that it had tarried until I reached the crude but sufficient asylum of the shelter. There's nothing quite like a nice rain when you are sitting comfortable and dry in a shelter. As darkness began to swallow the tiny hollow in which the shelters lay, I heard from the twin railroad tracks an old Iron Horse bellow out its alarm as it went thundering and shuddering through the valley where just hours ago I had walked.

As I lay there watching and listening to the sounds of night, I recalled the time that Dream Weaver and I were awakened in this very shelter, during the early morning hours, by the sounds of howling coyotes as they passed through the ravine. That night, when I heard them, I whispered to Dream Weaver to stir him, but he was already awake. We lay breathlessly listening to their eerie and doleful trademark sound, which seemed so close to us. Slowly, the animals began to move away, and the howling became fainter. I listened as long as I could, and fell asleep waiting for more. That night I gained a deeper appreciation for the sounds that nighttime can bring – sounds that cannot be heard during the din of day while light seemingly keeps at bay such creatures of mystery.

Tonight, the rain seemed to quiet the forest. Fixing the fire once more, I closed my eyes, and fell asleep with the sound of the pouring rain still dancing all around.

Day Two

With the dawning of day came memories of a restless night. Trying to get comfortable overnight on the hard shelter floor had not been easy. The first night out on the trail is usually like that for me. Although my mind might be trail-ready, my body takes some additional time to adjust to the lack of the daily comforts that I so adore. However, in a day or two, I knew that any discomfort I may feel at night will be overshadowed by sheer exhaustion, and sleep will not become so elusive.

As I made breakfast and leisurely packed my things, my mind went back several years to a time when my friends and I awoke quite early in this shelter. Dream Weaver had graciously commissioned himself to make our morning coffee. Into my waiting cup, he poured a liberal portion, and I stepped to the edge of the shelter to enjoy a freshly made mug of coffee against the peaceful backdrop of a new day.

As I sipped from my cup, however, my picture perfect morning took a sour twist. The coffee did not taste like coffee as I remembered it, and with no small amount of difficulty, I swallowed the mouthful. Week Knees, who had just tasted his coffee, and who did not labor under the same stringent laws of etiquette, spewed it out like a breeching whale.

"Argh! What did you put in the coffee?" Week Knees cried, shaking his head in vain to rid the curse from his palate.

"Yeah, what's in this stuff?" I asked with a pucker.

"Oh, come on guys," Dream Weaver innocently pleaded. "There's nothing wrong with the coffee."

It was not a time for cute trail names. "Dave, I'm telling ya – there's something wrong with the coffee!" I said between the spasms that were contorting my mouth.

Dream Weaver was truly suspect of our reactions, but decided to investigate our claims. The recipe for instant coffee is not complicated and he had long since committed it to memory. But upon inspecting the ingredients Dream Weaver realized his mistake.

"Ah – guys," he sheepishly announced, "I think I know what the problem is. You see… I didn't boil *water* for the coffee."

Having known and hiked with Dream Weaver for years, we began to prepare ourselves for the worst.

"I think that when I reached for my water bottle I instead grabbed my bottle of orange Gatorade by mistake."

Week Knees and I spat a lot that day. The sour taste of fruity java was hard to shake, and for many days afterward, I shivered whenever I recalled the un-enticing flavor of orange Gatorade coffee.

I was fitting my backpack for this day's journey, when I saw my new friend emerge from his nylon cocoon. He told me that he had had a good night, and that his tent held fast in the rain. I waved goodbye as I started on my way, and he told me that he would probably see me at the end of the day at the next shelter area.

From the moment one returns to the trail from the Ohiopyle Shelters, and turns north, a significant ascent is faced. It is probably the most enduring climb on the entire

Laurel Highlands Hiking Trail. For a mile and a quarter, the trail steadily rises about 1100 feet, earning its unofficial namesake, "Heart Attack Hill." Although Laurel Ridge Park Manager Sam Bowers could not recall anyone actually having a heart attack on the hill, he told me that it had induced some heat stroke casualties.

Though the rain had ceased, and the day was still young, the air was already filled with a desperate humidity. The woods had a steamy presence about it, resembling more of a tropical rain forest than a western Pennsylvania woodland. I did not climb 50 yards before becoming saturated in my own sweat, which dripped from my forehead, ran down my arms, and streamed over my legs.

As a general rule, I do not wear cotton clothing on the trail. Cotton absorbs water, and in cold conditions can increase the risk of hypothermia. In warmer weather, while hypothermia may not be a threat, wet cotton garments can become heavy and uncomfortable. Synthetic clothing, like polyester, is preferred because it does not retain as much water. Against these rules I had worn a cotton T-shirt today, but was glad that I did. It became drenched and felt good pressing against my body, absorbing the heat, and creating a refreshing feeling whenever the wind blew across it.

The morning sun, still on the rise, had not yet peeked into the ravine. With the heavy, summertime canopy, and lack of direct sunlight, the trail remained a darkened path. Occasionally I would pass small openings in the foliage where the limbs and branches sent their entanglements elsewhere. This allowed unbroken shafts of light to pierce through.

From these leafy windows I could peek outside the muggy umbrage, and look upon the exterior of Cave Hollow. Like a groove mistakenly cut by the wayward tool of a carpenter, the ravine seems to have been crudely cleaved into the side of the hill. The gash looked like a deep and painful wound. Yet, the sound of running water pouring over rocks somewhere far beneath me, sounded like a cool balm sent to soothe the mountain's ache.

As one might guess, 'Heart Attack Hill' is not an easy climb. In minutes I was breathing very hard, and by the time I would reach the summit, I could only take about a dozen steps before pausing to catch my breath. There was a time, not many years ago, when I would actually run up some of these hills – with a full pack – just to do it. I do not run anymore, but I still enjoy the feel of a good hard climb. The sensation of blood being pushed through veins to oxygen-starved muscles, as the heart and lungs work feverishly to fuel a desire that the mind has fastened upon, is truly exhilarating.

I do not have the body of a twenty-year-old man anymore. But through visits to the local gym, I do what I can to retard the affects of aging. There, I am often reminded of the chasm between what the mind wants to do, and what the body is capable of. This became apparent to me not long before this trip as I was at the gym doing some cardio and abdominal exercises.

One abdominal exercise involves the use the of "gravity boots." They are not really boots, but sleeves with hooks that strap around the ankles. The wearer reaches to an overhead bar, swings the legs upward, and hooks the sleeves to the bar. Suspended upside down from the feet, the athlete does crunches, or sit-ups to strengthen the "abs."

The gym had set up a bar between two uprights that were positioned not too far apart from each other. I had performed the exercise there many times without any trouble. Then, they moved the overhead bar to another station where the uprights were placed further apart. On this particular day, I decided I would employ the gravity boots for some pre-hike crunches. The gym was filled with younger, stronger men, and quite honestly, I felt that this gave me a great way to prove that I was not beyond my prime.

Swinging my legs upward I hooked the sleeves to the overhead bar and unraveled myself until I was hanging completely upside down. I then executed ten very sharp crunches that I was simply convinced must have been impressive to any onlooker. They felt good and I knew I had some more in me. So, to give any possible audience their money's worth, I did about five more, deep, upside down crunches. I relaxed to a hanging position and thought that two more would really be the *coup de grâce* for this fine exhibition of elegance and strength. No doubt the young bucks standing around the gym would be duly impressed. So, I reached deep inside of me and pulled out two more crunches. They were not as good as I had hoped for, but I got through them and returned to my suspended position. I hung there for a second or so, and then curled myself upward to reach the bar and make a graceful dismount. But, to my great alarm, I found that I did not have the strength to reach the bar. The last of my energy had been spent. When doing this before I simply reached to the vertical side support bars, and, taking them in my hands, lifted my feet off the bar. I anxiously looked to both sides of me now, and saw that the support bars were too far from my reach.

Now, this was a dilemma of disheartening proportions. I tried again to reach the overhead bar, but this attempt was even poorer than the one before. I returned to the upside down position and thought for a moment about my predicament. While I was thinking of what to do, I tried looking comfortable, there, upside down on the bar – as if I were taking an afternoon break at the office water cooler, or thumbing through a magazine in the doctor's office waiting room. I yawned once, and stretched casually, showing no outside sign of my concern. But, inside, I was beginning to feel ill with the unpleasant reality of my situation.

It was pointless to attempt again to reach the top bar. My salvation would come through one of two means: ask someone for help, or wait until the gym closes and ask the cleaning person to dial 911. I could not see the clock from where I hanged, but I knew that the latter solution would require at least several more hours of suspension. Aside from the obvious physical demands of hanging upside down for that long, I would also be faced with the annoying queries, unkind gestures, and uncomfortable conversation that were certain to ensue.

To my left stood a weight lifter whose first name I knew. He is a strong man with arms as large as my thighs.

"Hey Mike," I called to him. Quizzically, he looked my way. Not wanting to announce my dilemma to everyone in listening range, I motioned him over as if I had found something of incredible worth and wanted to show it to him. He strolled over and bent down with the same puzzled look.

"I can't seem to reach the bar," I gasped.

"That bar?" the strong man asked, gesturing to the bar that I was suspended from. A faint smile appeared at the corners of his mouth.

"Yes," I weakly responded. "Can ya give me a hand?"

Mike placed one of his large arms beneath my back as I gave a feeble lunge toward the overhead bar. Suddenly a surge of power came from beneath me. I sailed through the air and grasped the bar, fearing that if I did not, I might flip over to the other side.

"Got it," I muttered in a manner that I hoped would conceal my embarrassment. I seized the bar as if I did this all of the time and quietly dismounted. Since that occasion, I have performed my crunches from the floor where I am certain that I can always make good my escape.

The trail continued its steep ascent out of the ravine, testing the oatmeal I had for breakfast. My muscles strained beneath the weight of my pack, and against the incline of the hillside. In spite of its steepness, however, most hikers will agree that they would rather hike up a hill like this, than down it. Hiking down a very steep mountain can really be hard on the knees, especially when a heavy pack is attached to your back.

Less than one mile from the Bidwell Shelters, as I still struggled with my ascent, I crossed the invisible boundary separating Fayette and Somerset Counties. I would cross back into Fayette County once more, near the eighteen-mile post, and then follow the trail as it wanders back and forth between Somerset, Westmoreland, and Cambria Counties for the remainder of the walk.

Finally, I reached the summit. Quite suddenly the trail leveled off, pretending as if it had always been so gracious and kind. There is a very nice view on top of the hill, from the west side of the trail. Sugarloaf Knob, looking like a swollen lump on the mountain across the expanse, is easy to spot from the top. I stepped out of the woods, and onto the rocks that litter this scenic overlook.

Taking off my backpack, I sat down and examined the view. I also kept an eye out for snakes that might be sunning themselves on the rocks. In particular, I was concerned with the kind of snake that rattles.

Just about a mile north of this spot I had my first encounter with a rattlesnake some years before. I was hiking alone and walking south toward the Ohiopyle

Shelters. Week Knees was hiking north from Ohiopyle. We had planned to meet at the shelter. I was moving merrily along the trail with not a care in the world, when suddenly, out of the corner of my eye, I spotted something moving across the path. It coiled rapidly and I probably took one or two more steps before I realized what it was. By that time, the snake was rattling feverishly. It was in a tight coil with its head low, and its tail raised slightly – just like the photographs I had seen.

It was not very long, but was as thick as a logging chain. I was only a few feet from it when I realized what it was. I jumped back pretty quickly, giving the noisy reptile plenty of room to feel comfortable. I walked back a few yards, waiting for it to leave, but it seemed content to wait me out. Since it was directly on the path where I intended to walk, I decided to circumnavigate the snake, and walk through the brush around the trail. I figured that as long as I could hear it ratting, then I knew where it was.

As I was pushing myself through the entanglement beside the trail, the rattling suddenly stopped. I became even more frightened because I no longer knew the location of the snake. I pushed harder through the thicket and reached the trail on the other side in a run. From that time on, I have walked with a little more consideration for where my feet are placed.

The Timber Rattlesnake of Western Pennsylvania is generally a timid thing. It prefers to make a quiet retreat rather than stand its ground against humans. I met a thru-hiker on the Appalachian Trail in West Virginia who told me that a rattlesnake struck at him when he surprised it on a rock ledge. But, he said, the strike fell short, causing him to believe that the snake never really intended to bite him at all – just send a clear message to stay away.

There is another poisonous snake that lives near the

Laurel Highlands Hiking Trail – the Northern Copperhead. The Northern Copperhead and the Timber Rattlesnake both belong to the same pit viper family. This family of snakes is notable for their arrowhead-shaped heads. The Copperhead does not rattle, but can be identified by the hourglass patterns of dark patches on its back.

I am told that these snakes can also be identified by their vertical pupils. That information, however, is absolutely useless to me. I can scarcely imagine that the next time I come upon a snake in the wild, and, being unable determine if it is a threat to me or not, will simply drop down on my hands and knees to gander into its eyes. No, I think I would prefer to walk away in a dark cloud of ignorant uncertainty than try to identify the tiny pupils of a snake's eyes.

Sam Bowers at Laurel Ridge Park told me that to his knowledge, no one has ever been bitten by a poisonous snake on the Laurel Highlands Hiking Trail. That is an impressive record, and I have no desire to challenge it. I was informed that rattlesnake sightings are increasing as never before. Although it is possible that the rattlesnake population is on the rise, it should be noted that the number of visitors who might see a snake has also increased.

In their 1991 hiking guide to the Laurel Highlands Hiking Trail, the Sierra Club of Western Pennsylvania and the Western Pennsylvania Conservancy reported that Dr. Eleanor Morris, who practiced medicine in nearby Jones Mills, never even saw a poisonous snake bite case in her twenty-five years of practice. However, one of the founding fathers of the Turkeyfoot area, William Lanning, is known to have died from the bite of a rattlesnake sometime after settling here in 1770.

If one is traveling north on the trail, then this rocky ledge offers the last view of the Youghigheny River as it washes along its course. Unlike most North American rivers, the Yough flows north. It is truly a river in its own right: that is, it is not borne out of another river, or larger body of water.

In Tim Palmer's book, *Youghiogheny: Appalachian River*, the author traced the river to its birthing place, located on Backbone Mountain in Maryland, near the West Virginia line. Following the Yough on foot, he watched it narrow to just a trickle until he finally stood at the base of Hoyes Crest. There he observed:

> *The Youghiogheny at this altitude is a damp spot in the bottom of a Maryland ravine. As we press upward, sink-sized pools of water appear now and then with drops of current running through... I see where it begins in a cavity like a tiny cirque, fifteen feet across... And right at the back of the cirque, tight against the mountain, is a spring measuring one foot across, two inches deep, and edged with the yellow pollen of May.*

From that mountain-spring cradle, the two-inch deep puddle begins its course; dipping into West Virginia, and then returning to Maryland, while gaining speed and volume as it enters Pennsylvania. It stretches 132 miles, from its southern incipience to where it finds its end in McKeesport, Pennsylvania. There the Yough pours into the Monongahela River at 3,000 cubic feet of water per second.

The water that I looked at from these rocks has quite a journey before it. After reaching McKeesport, and splashing into the Monongahela River, it will flow northward to join the Ohio River in downtown Pittsburgh,

Pennsylvania. From there it will travel westward to just south of Cairo, Illinois, where it meets the mighty Mississippi River. The Mississippi takes the water on a southern ride until it pours into the wide-open waters of the Gulf of Mexico. It is a wondrous thing to consider that the tiny puddle of water at the foot of Hoyes Crest in Maryland begins a bouncy, northward journey, only to end up, after 2,082 twisty miles, to the south far behind it.

Taking advantage of the openness of this high peak, I retrieved my cell phone from my pack, and placed a call to my sister to wish her a happy birthday. I left a message on her answering machine and turned off the phone. My sister had the good fortune of being born into a home with three older brothers who were anxious for something new in their lives. We were thankful that our parents brought us this new toy, and we each had our share of adventures with her. From strapping a plastic helmet on her head and pushing her around the floor in one of our toy trucks, to stuffing her in a sleeping bag and swinging her around in great circles, banging lamps and walls with our lively bundle – we were eager to show her what we had found to be fun in our world.

My younger brother once sprained her wrist when he dropped her to the ground; I got her foot stuck in the moving spokes of my bicycle wheel, and my older brother ran over her with a farm tractor. I suppose it should not be considered a strange thing that she is the only sibling who did not remain close to home after high school.

With my break over, I returned my pack to its place on my body, and stepped off the bebouldered, sunlit ridge to rejoin the shaded footpath of the Laurel Highlands Hiking Trail. Immediately, my senses were flooded with the richness of the woods. The previous night's rain had pristinely washed the forest, revealing a purity that baffled the senses. The canopy above glistened with filtered light waves that rained upon my upturned, astonished face. Ferns that covered the ground rolled back and forth in the wind like waves atop the ocean, spilling and splashing beads of water on the soil beneath, softening it for my anxious boots. The air in this oxygen-rich environment tasted as unadulterated and clean as any I ever drew in. This is the wonder of hiking, unfurling in all of its glory, raining generously upon anyone who desires to find it.

The trail leveled off nicely and the walk from atop the ridge became much easier. I was amazed as to how open the trail was. Occasionally, a fallen tree might stretch across the trail, but mostly the southern section of the trail offers a wide and comfortable path to follow. Walking it with such ease one can never know the incredible labor that was put into designing and maintaining it.

The trail was planned by Pennsylvania State Park personnel, and headed by Robert "Bob" Hufman and Jerry Yocum. Work on the trail began in 1970, and was completed in 1976. Building a trail where there is no trail is not easy work. Sam Bowers told me that the first thing to be done is to ribbon off or mark the trail. Then crews come through with chainsaws clearing the way of trees, branches, shrubbery, and logs. Next, with the use of fire rakes, shovels, bars, and mattocks, crews begin the backbreaking task of raking clear the trail of roots, rocks, and smaller obstructions.

And then there are the bridges. During a conversation with Donna and Sam at Laurel Ridge Park, she encouraged him to boast about the fine bridges that he makes. Sam smiled bashfully, and described the making of the many bridges that hikers cross on the Laurel Highlands Hiking Trail. First a red oak is selected. Sam said that they used to pick one far from the trail so the stump would not be visible. But, he added laughingly, they now pick the closest red oak they can find because it is not easy dragging a tree through the woods with just a single helper.

After felling a red oak, Sam cuts it to size so that it can adequately span the creek. He then runs a chalk line down the middle and splits the tree. The secret in getting the two halves to fit closely together, he shared, is to edge the insides of both logs so they fit flush with one another. Rocks are selected to be the supporting pillars, and the two halves are tightly fitted together atop the rocks. There are many wood bridges on the Laurel Highlands Hiking Trail. Each one represents hours of work, many drops of sweat, and trained know-how.

Passing the 11-mile marker, I reached Maple Summit Road. I was hungry, and since I had walked so long in the deep shade of the woods, this opening provided the perfect spot to relax, enjoy lunch, and take in the sun. I lowered my pack to the ground, and leaned it against a small oak. Withdrawing my lunch from the pack, I sat down on the ground and comfortably leaned against my backpack, stretching my legs before me. While eating lunch, I could hear loud music and voices coming from the nearby State parking area just off Maple Summit Road. It sounded like a small group of people might be preparing to hike, but I did not see anyone walk to the trail.

Once, Week Knees and I were hiking this section of the trail. We were both moving north with Week Knees a few minutes walk ahead of me. As I rounded a bend in the trail, I saw Week Knees standing and talking with an elderly gentleman. Approaching them, Week Knees mouthed toward me the words "he's lost."

It seemed the gentleman was hiking with a group of senior citizens from out of state. They each had selected their own route to take on the trail, and were instructed to return to the parking area of Maple Summit Road when finished. The man originally hiked north then turned around to return to the parking lot.

As Week Knees examined the man's hand-drawn map, he discovered that the gentleman had mistakenly crossed Maple Summit Road, and was now moving away from his party. The man was visibly shaken. He knew that he was lost, but he could not find his mistake, and therefore, was continuing to hike south, putting even more distance between his group and himself. We invited him to walk with us back to the road, and he quite anxiously accepted our offer. Week Knees and I were both surprised as to the quick pace of this elderly hiker.

It is an easy thing to get lost. The challenge is to remain calm when you realize your situation. Through failure, I learned just how important it is to keep calm in the woods.

When I was about sixteen, I had gone archery hunting with my father and older brother. They stationed themselves at the edge of a forest near an open field. My father gave me clear instructions: walk along the side of the woods; make a 90 degree turn into the trees; walk a short distance, and then turn another 90 degrees back toward the field where they were positioned. The purpose of the venture was to flush out any deer toward them.

I successfully executed the first turn and was nearing the place where I needed to turn again when suddenly I came upon several deer. I launched an arrow after one of the fleeing animals and, as usual, missed my mark by several feet. I went looking for my arrow and spent several minutes digging around the underbrush. When I arose to continue my course, I found myself disoriented. I had forgotten from which direction I had been walking, and to where I was heading. Instead of carefully retracing my steps and making a solid determination of which direction to take, I selected a route that seemed right to me and began to move that way.

As the minutes passed I started to become alarmed that I had not reached the edge of the woods. I continued walking until soon my walk became a run. At one point my hat tumbled off a small ledge while I was scaling some rocks. I had reached such a state of panic by that time that I nearly did not go back to retrieve it. I was completely lost and could not think clearly. Fortunately, my father was not very trusting of his son's woodcraft and came looking for me. As I was resting against a tree feeling quite overwhelmed, I suddenly heard him calling out my name. The relief I felt has never been rivaled. Lesson learned: remain calm.

Maple Summit Road is a hard-surfaced road, cutting southeast across the Laurel Highlands Hiking Trail. Shortly after crossing paths with the trail, it seamlessly becomes the intensely shaded Jersey Hollow Road as it moves toward Ursina, Pennsylvania. About five miles east of where I was having lunch is The Turkeyfoot Baptist Church – otherwise known as The Old Jersey Church. This is the oldest Baptist church west of the Allegheny Mountains, and the earliest of all denominations in Somerset County.

In 1770, a group of hardy settlers left New Jersey in search of more fertile soil where they could raise crop for their families and stock. They migrated to Turkeyfoot – a name given to the area because the Casselman River, Laurel Hill Creek, and the Youghiogheny River, converge together in a manner resembling that of a turkey's foot.

Five years after the families arrived, they formed a congregation that met in one another's homes for worship. In January of 1788, the settlers built a two-story log structure that served as a church and school. Those were still difficult, dangerous times. Worshipers attended church with rifles, and guards were posted at the corners to protect them from Indian attack. Robert Holliday, a fine historian, now living in Confluence, Pennsylvania, told me that he believed rifle slots were built into the original church structure to shoot from if necessary. The original log cabin was replaced in 1838, but was reportedly destroyed by fire thirty-nine years later. The building that now stands in its stead was raised in 1877.

I have visited the old church on several occasions, and walked its perimeter. Although the church no longer has an active congregation, the structure and grounds are surprisingly well maintained. On more than one occasion I've brushed away the cobwebs and flaking white paint that decorate the windowsills. Peeking through the clear glass windows and scanning the three rows of pews I have cupped my hands over my eyes and with my imagination tried to peer into the first log structure. I have pictured the church being filled with late 18th century country folk who momentarily left their struggles to gather together for inspiration, forgiveness, and renewal, within the sanctity of this old wood building.

Men, as hard as the timber they sawed, brought their wives, who were no less equal to the task of hard settler life, and their children to this small wooded chapel, and offered their worship. Sunday School, weddings, meetings, funerals, and picnics were undoubtedly the gathering events that brought the faithful to meet at this now historical landmark.

On the north side of the church is a large, well-kept cemetery. A stroll through the rolling polyandrium clearly shows that mourners continue to tread the grounds, laying to rest their loved ones, and faithfully decorating the graves of those already at slumber. When I last passed through, I found numerous headstones marking the plot where a person was buried, and beside them a vacant plot waiting for his or her spouse and the first day of their eternal bliss together.

On the south side of the church there is an older cemetery. In it I not only found the final resting place of many Civil War veterans, but also noted the headstones bearing the nearly forgotten names of those buried there who fought in this country's struggle for independence during the Revolutionary War. Astonishingly, some of these old markers are very well preserved. The gravestone of Mary Rush, who departed this life in 1826, is brilliantly conserved. It clearly bears testimony of her faith, and a hint of drollery, as it shares in stanza:

> *Though greedy worms devour my skin,*
> *And gnaw my wasting flesh,*
> *When God shall build my bones again,*
> *He'll clothe them all afresh*

Other tombstones have not fared so well against the harsh mountain elements. Their names have faded away like the once vivid memories of the dearly departed. Some markers bear no semblance of monuments; rather, they appear as simple fieldstones turned upward. These seem to struggle to keep atop the encroaching soil and continue to bear mute testimony of those interred beneath their charge.

Once each summer the parishioners of the Confluence Baptist Church bring their brooms, buckets and rags into the church to clean it. On the second Sunday of each August the doors are opened for an annual service. Years ago I attended one of these services. There, with the Confluence Baptist congregation, I gladly worshipped in the historical church. The pews are hard, short, and built low to the floor. But they get the job done and it was inspiring to sit inside the old sanctuary.

We cracked open old hymnals that burst forth with a melancholic must. Our voices then were joined with those now silent; singing together songs of faith and hope. As we sang together, and the congregation shared stories about the church and her people, I had the very real sense of being involved in something sacred. It was as if I were sitting not just with the Confluence Baptist congregation, but with all of the worshippers who had ever entered the Jersey Church's doors.

As the service proceeded, I looked above at the church's flat ceiling, and around at its faded walls. Oh, if they could be given but for a minute to talk, I wondered! Would they tell me of the myriad of sermons that must have been preached from the now lonely wooden pulpit? Would they speak of the men and women, who having been pushed to their limits in this rugged place, found inspiration somewhere in the words of an old country preacher? Would they share of the weary preachers who poured themselves into their messages never knowing the spark they created, or the fire that that spark ignited? Would they recall the splash of water upon the eager heads of its catechumens, or of joyful bells sounding at weddings? Would they toll over its fallen?

Sitting beside me was an old timer. He must have been entertaining the same thoughts. As my mind wondered he gestured out of the window at a mammoth tree and whispered with a smile, "If that old oak could talk. They grow slow, you know. Very slow."

I finished lunch along Maple Summit Road and then gathered my things. The rest and refreshment did me well. Accompanied by a light rain, I crossed the road and reentered the woods. In less than one mile I crossed Cranberry Road. This is a twisting gravel road that cuts through State Game Lands No. 111. About one tenth of a mile to the west of the trail, at the base of a small, forested hill, is a stone and concrete structure known as Schwiebenz's Spring.

While walking along the trail on another occasion, I had strolled down to the spring and found two men drawing water from it. Anxious to learn a little history of the spring I eagerly approached them.

"Hello!" I called out, being just as concerned with not startling them as I was with greeting them.

"Howdy," the taller man said as he stood up from over a bucket of water. He was dressed in very worn blue jeans and a blue flannel shirt buttoned to the collar. His hands had the appearance of those that were often performing some greasy job. I sensed that they were seldom clean. His ball cap was deeply soiled and the bill no longer held its form. He looked to be in his seventies but with the layers of dirt it was hard to be certain.

"Hey there," the other man said while still bending over a container of water. He was dressed much like the taller man and seemed a few years younger.

They had about a dozen plastic containers and buckets sitting around. The shorter man was dipping water from the spring and pouring it into a container set nearby. The taller man was lifting the filled containers to the back of an early model, primer-gray Chevrolet truck parked nearby.

"Is that water any good?" I asked.

"You betcha'," the shorter man replied proudly. "Won't find water any place better!"

I looked in one of the filled buckets near my feet and saw a few insects and other specs floating on top.

"What do you use to filter it?" I asked.

The taller man seemed confused. "Filter it? Hell!" he said. "This water comes straight from the ground. It don't need no filterin'.'"

"Do you use it for drinking?" I asked.

Just as soon as I spoke the words I wished that I had not. I could tell by the pained looks on their faces that my question had hurt. I had assumed that they might be using it to water the garden, do their laundry, or feed animals. But their facial reactions told me that I had just insulted the integrity of this fine spring.

"Of course we use it for drinkin'," the shorter man said while reaching his dirty hand beneath the ball cap to scratch his balding scalp. "This is the best tastin' water anywhere."

"Any idea who built this spring, or how long it's been here?" I asked to change the subject. I figured that these two men were natives of the area and could answer some of my questions.

Squinting his eyes and scrunching his face to help his recall, the shorter man said slowly, "Well, now, that I can't say."

"Have no idea 'bout that," the taller flannel-shirted man chipped in. "This spring has been here as long as I've been in these parts."

"Then you've been coming here for a long time to get your water?" I asked, trying to get a feel for the age of the spring and my interviewees.

"Ever since we've moved to these parts!" the older man said. Then turning to his counterpart he asked, "How long 'as that been?"

"Oh, I reckon we've been livin' 'round here for two or three years now," the younger man replied.

The encounter with the two men did not reveal much in terms of history of the spring. However, a conversation later with local historian Bob Holliday revealed that the Works Progress Association (WPA) built the spring during the Depression years. The WPA was part of President

Franklin D. Roosevelt's "New Deal" program designed to bring relief and economical reform to the country.

About two miles beyond Schwiebenz Spring on Cranberry Road, one can reach what I have found to be one of the most thrilling sites in Fayette County: ten, 210-foot windmills. Completed in November of 2001, these intimidating structures churn out electricity for customers in Pennsylvania, Maryland, and New Jersey. Their spinning blades span 231 feet from tip to tip, and it seems they never stop turning in the breezes that continually shift across the hilltop.

The windmills are lined up across the top of a rolling ridge of green grass. Each time that I approach I find myself catching my breath at the sight of the sheer magnitude of these gentle giants. A dirt road leads closely past the towering, white wind-seekers, allowing an impressive view. From the roadway one can usually see cattle leisurely grazing at their base seemingly unaware of these remarkable landmarks. Only when it is truly quiet outside can you hear an almost indiscernible whir-whir-whirring as the blades cut through the air. From this rolling hill, harnessed wind now lights a child's nightlight, warms a cold house on a winter's night, and percolates a pot of coffee on a kitchen stove.

Approximately twenty miles away, these windmills have six sister structures near Berlin in Somerset County. I have often visited that location too, where one can stand unbelievably close to the seemingly topless white pillars. Every time I approach them I sense a wonder that causes me to shrink back beneath their towering height. Interestingly, a plaque at the Somerset site recognizes Mr. Nicholas Humber who "made critical contributions to the planning and completion of the wind projects" at both of these locations. Sadly, on September 11, 2001, Mr. Humber lost his life while aboard American Airlines Flight 11 that was crashed into the Pentagon.

About 300 feet below the Cranberry Windmills is Cranberry Glade Lake. It is a popular fishing spot managed by the State Game Commission. A boat launch makes it easy to set out a rowboat to enjoy a day on the lake, threshing the waters for that elusive catch-of-the-day.

After crossing Cranberry Glade Road, I continued my trek north, passing the 12-mile marker. This placed me at the halfway point of the day's hike. I soon came across the remainder of a very large conifer tree on the east side of the trail – now sheared off about 15 feet from the roots. Scattered everywhere were splinters of wood - some pieces as far away as 50 yards. The debris-strewn field plainly testified of a brutal lightning strike.

Lightning is a dangerous element of backpacking that cannot be eliminated, even by the most careful planning. Storms can brew quickly in mountainous regions. Laurel Hill is no exception. Hiking through electrical storms can be unnerving, especially when you are walking atop a ridge like on the Laurel Highlands Hiking Trail. Years before, I had the opportunity to speak with a young man who hiked the entire Appalachian Trail. He told me that of all the dangers and risks of the trail, the one that frightened him the most was lightning. He related for me a night when he huddled in his tent in the middle of a fierce electrical storm. He said that there was nothing he could do but wait it out and pray that no electrical charge was directed his way. It was his most unnerving night in the wild.

Once, while camping in Nebraska, I witnessed one of the most spectacular electrical storms that I had ever seen. Having been accustomed to Pennsylvania electrical storms and its lightning bolts, I did not expect anything different. But in this storm I saw lightning that curled, twisted, and sliced through the air in a *horizontal* fashion. I was struck with tremendous awe and fear. Tornado warnings were broadcasted that night, and I heard that a funnel cloud touched down about thirty miles north of where my tent was pitched. It was a night that I can still vividly recall.

Looking at the frayed and shattered pieces of wood and bark at my feet on the trail reminded me of the irresistible strength of a frighteningly unpredictable force that can be easily and suddenly unleashed.

Moving northward, I passed through a forest whose floor alternated between thick lush ferns and softened mulch that was carefully tended by the falling needles of towering pine trees. Each step, it seemed, brought a new sight, or a new smell, something to admire, or something to smile at. The sounds of the forest also vacillated. At times the singing birds and chirping chipmunks, coupled with the creaking trees being bent by the wind, created a symphony of sound. While at other times, the path led me to places of perfect silence. Here only the muffled sound of my boots falling across the well-worn path could be heard above my labored breathing.

I walked past streams and creeks that were lovingly embraced by blooming mountain laurel and leafy rhododendron. So thickly did they reach out their branches that the water could not even be seen. Instead, it was only heard as it washed over ancient rocks, and dripped into unseen crannies. And always the smells of the forest wafted upward like the sweet incense of a flickering candle being perpetually burned before its Creator.

I passed a fallen tree with its upturned roots gripping a boulder near a stream. It seemed that the roots had not gone deeply into the ground, but only ensnared the large rock. Probably at the insistence of a stormy wind the tree toppled, not being properly rooted, and with it the rock was torn from the ground. Yet, in spite of its new and permanent resting place at the bottom of the forest floor, the tree continued to thrive. Its green branches reached upward like the arms of a fallen child yearning for its mother.

My afternoon walk finally led me to one of my favorite places on the Laurel Highlands Hiking Trail. Just north of mile marker thirteen the trail crosses the breast of a body of water that is part of Twin Lakes. It is a man-made dam with duck boxes fastened to trees that jut out of the water. Just beyond the closest dam is another body of water that is not easily seen from the trail.

I sat down on the dam breast and leaned my backpack against the same small maple tree that had often cradled me along the shores of this body of water. This is an easy place to be. Here, the wind always seems to blow. On hot days the wind is cooled as it crosses the dam so that it reaches the tired hiker in a welcoming way. I withdrew some snacks from my pack and took advantage of the spot for some rest. Ducks were quacking out on the water, and occasionally a muted splash could be heard as a fish surfaced for a tasty floating insect. Water lapping at my feet brought to mind the soreness that I was beginning to feel from my southernmost extremities. Removing my shoes, I stretched my legs, and snuggled deeper into my backpack and the maple behind me. Pulling my cap down over my face to protect from insects, I closed my eyes and for a few minutes left the toil of my day for the pleasures of light slumber.

When the tiredness wore away and strength returned to my muscles, I gathered my things and started northward. Rounding the dam, I recalled a time when my companions and I were hiking south at this very spot. The sky was threatening rain but we had not donned our rain garments.

As we stood at the corner of the dam, we saw a cloudburst on the other side, which was rapidly moving in our direction. As one person, we dropped our packs and began pulling free our ponchos. The rain, looking like a wall of water, worked its way across the dam seemingly gaining speed toward our small group. Frantically, we worked at waterproofing our equipment and ourselves, all the while watching the edge of the rainstorm draw nearer until it overtook us like a speeding locomotive. Every time we now round the breast of the dam we remind one another of the collision we had with a wall of water.

Continuing northward, I pushed along the trail. At a small opening in the woods I spied a deer standing at alert attention. Its summer coat was deep red, and it looked beautiful against the green grass behind it. But it was too timid to allow me a long look, and it quickly and silently darted back into the woods.

As I neared the shelter area, and the end of the day's hike, I began to feel the common sensation of extreme tiredness. It seems to occur whenever you know the end of the trail is near. The last few miles are always the most difficult, and this day was no exception. But finally I saw the welcoming sight of the shelter area sign that points off the trail. Blue-colored blazes on the trees led me off the Laurel Highlands Hiking Trail to the 653 Shelter Area, named after Route 653 that intersects the trail just north of here. With great relief I hiked back to the lean-to that would be my home for the night, and dropped my backpack to the shelter floor. It felt good to be coddled by the stiff wood frame and planked floor of the shelter.

After a significant rest I gathered wood for a fire, and filled my canteens with water from the hand pump. A friendly blaze soon snapped and cracked in the fireplace, and I cooked dinner atop my portable stove. From the tin of my mess kit, I ate supper in comfortable silence. The succor of the meal and the heat of the fire refreshed me in remarkable ways.

I kept an eye out for my friend who I had met the night before, but as daylight dimmed I saw no one approach the camping area from the trail. He never appeared, and without explanation, I did not see him again on my hike.

I was visited, however, by the Park Ranger who rolled up in his SUV. The Rangers visit the shelter areas at night to collect fees from campers. I had already paid my fee, but he had come to collect dues from two other groups who were supposed to be camping in the shelters. He was not surprised at their absence. He told me that changing weather conditions and the harsh hiking terrain often send people back home.

We talked about the trail, and he told me stories of his experiences with both man and animal. He recounted an occasion when a group of Boy and Girl Scouts were camping together at the Ohiopyle Shelters. A black bear wandered into camp looking for food, and this so frightened the Boy Scouts that they called for a bus, which promptly arrived and carted them away. The Girl Scouts, however, bravely remained without further incident. The Ranger thought this to be very funny, and laughed at the story.

He also shared how he met a backpacker on the trail who woke up one night smelling what he described as a "wet dog." Looking out of the shelter, he saw a black bear licking the grill he had used to cook supper that night. The man told the Ranger that he was so frightened he could not get to sleep that night, and resorted to sleeping during the day, and hiking at night for fear of these animals.

After the Ranger departed, I repaired to my shelter and waited out the last threads of light stringing through the trees above. Fixing the fire one last time, I crawled into my sleeping bag and soundly fell asleep.

Day Three

The night passed in peaceful segments of deep slumber separated by brief entries of dazed arousal. During those periods of semi-wakefulness I found myself feeding the quenchless fire. But at some undefined moment I became aware of dawn's arrival. This was heralded by the sounds of morning life that began silencing the mysterious din of the nocturnal forest.

When sleep had completed its work within me I arose from my mat and set upon the task of boiling water for breakfast. Morning is a sacred time. And I have found no better way to venerate it on the trail then to fill my tin chalice with a steaming portion of black coffee, and reverently ease my way into the coming day with slow and steady sips.

When breakfast became a memory, I covered with ashes the last twinkling embers of the fire that had faithfully kept me company through the night. I then turned attention to making preparations for this day's walk. Moocher would be joining me for the day and forthcoming night, and I was looking forward to his company. Although I enjoy hiking in solitude, the evenings in camp are far more agreeable when in the company of others. Besides, Moocher always makes me laugh with his antics and dry sense of humor.

As I was packing my camping parcel, I heard a creaking noise that sounded like the water hand pump. Peeking around my lean-to, I observed a man walking toward the number five shelter from the water pump, and another man standing inside the shelter. Apparently after I had turned in for the night, they had arrived to camp. Perhaps they were of one of the parties that the Ranger was expecting.

I returned to packing my belongings and was nearly prepared to leave when I heard the sounds of approaching steps and a familiar voice calling out from behind the shelter, "Anyone home?"

"Yeah, but I'm not decent." I hollered back.

"When are you ever decent?" replied the voice as it drew closer.

I smiled; Moocher had arrived. He came around from the back of the shelter and greeted me with a wry grin.

"Where's your pack?" I asked noting that he carried nothing on his back.

"I decided not to bring one," he replied. "I figured that you'd bring enough of everything for both of us."

I knew that a joke lurked somewhere in this conversation. "Well, that's why we call you Moocher," I retorted, smiling along with him.

I lifted my pack to my back and buckled it in place. After two days of hiking I had hoped that it would feel a bit lighter – it did not. I took a hold of my trekking poles, and glanced back at the shelter making certain I had packed everything.

"Okay, let's boogie," I said.

We started walking away from the shelters. I kept an eye out for Moocher's backpack but did not see it anywhere. I hated to ask about it again. Clearly he had set the bait out for me, and though I was curious, I need not appear too anxious to figure out what was going on.

We walked past shelter number five. Whoever it was that I had seen earlier had already vacated without a trace.

Following the blue-blazed trail out of the shelter area we turned north on the Laurel Highlands Hiking Trail and began our trek. Immediately we hit a very steep, albeit short climb. In moments I was panting hard.

"Okay, where's your pack?" I asked between gasps. The curiosity got the better of me.

"I told you;" he said, "I didn't bring one."

I knew it was a joke, but I felt it was unfair that I was working so hard to make this climb while he effortlessly skipped up the rocks.

"Well, lookie here!" Moocher exclaimed as we reached the top of the hill. "Someone left a backpack along the trail! I wonder if it fits me?"

He bent down, picked up his backpack and slung it to his back, "Yepper. Fits like a glove. I think I'll keep it."

I rolled my eyes. Moocher had left his backpack at the top of the hill when he came down to meet me so that he did not have to carry it back up. It was a smart move, and I would probably have done the same. But the unwritten code that governs conversation between us did not allow me to congratulate him on his wise choice, or admit that he had me going.

"Well, then we better get out of here before the owner comes back looking for it," I said.

"Nah, we won't have to worry about that. I left a note on the ground where the pack was with your name and phone number on it."

Yes, hiking with a companion has its advantages.

As we began to walk, Moocher told me that this was the only section of the trail that he had never walked. He explained that at the close of the day he will have finally hiked the entire Laurel Highlands Hiking Trail. Although done in sections, he was excited to have it finally completed.

We soon reached Route 653. This is a hardtop Pennsylvania State Road; one of the four significant passageways leading west out of Somerset County over Laurel Hill Mountain. Its eastern hand rests in Garrett, Pennsylvania, and it runs for approximately twenty-six miles to its western terminus in Normalville, Pennsylvania.

Like most modern-day roads, Route 653 is mostly made up of pre-existing passageways that have been linked together to form a highway route. Often the histories of these sections do not share the same past. The remote section of Route 653 that we were standing on in Springfield Township seems to have little to do with the section of 653 at the eastern end – which is Main Street in Garrett – except that they both are part of the same roadway.

The section of Route 653 that breaks in two the Laurel Highlands trail is known as Jim Mountain Road. It is named after the Mountain family who once lived in the area. Before its current name, the road was known as Clay Pike Road – so called for its un-piked surface covered in dusty clay. Like many of the roads in the region, Clay Pike began as a simple path through the woods, most likely made by the Indians.

The early settlers found the path and began following it over the mountain. Eventually, the path was widened to form a road. The original Clay Pike (sometimes known as Mud Pike) ran from Berlin, Pennsylvania, to Normalville (then known as Springfield). The road provided good passage over the mountain, and was used extensively in the early days. It was surveyed as a road in 1810, and completed around 1820. Franklin Ellis, who wrote *History of Fayette County*, recorded that nearly two centuries ago, standing at this very place, one could have witnessed hundreds of horses, mules, cattle, sheep, and hogs being driven over the thoroughfare each week.

The great trafficking of livestock created business opportunities for those who settled in the area. Large barns were built to provide relief to the weary hoofed-traveler, and places of rest were provided to their drivers for a reasonable fee. When the B & O Railroad was completed, the old Clay Pike was not as sorely needed, but it did not fade from existence. It has been continually improved, and stands today as a comfortable, scenic ride over Laurel Hill. The Laurel Ridge State Park Office is located about 100 yards east of where the trail crosses Route 653.

Before crossing the road, Moocher and I set down our packs and walked west. About a quarter of a mile off of the trail, on Route 653, is a most peculiar find. At the edge of the road, covered with grass and gravel, is the old "Indian Stone." This stone bears the carved profile of an Indian in a feathered headdress. At one time a pipe could be seen in the Indian's mouth. But the pipe is now mostly eroded away.

The rock is level with the road surface, and there are no markings to show where to find it. Most travelers are probably not even aware of the relic as they drive quickly by on this well-maintained highway. Finding the stone is not easy - finding the stone's history is even more difficult. The Somerset County Archaeology Society referred me to Mr. Tom Cramer, (no relation to this author) who seems to have done the most extensive research on the stone. Tom has dubbed the stone "Sentinel" because it seems to be standing watch along the road. He provided me with copies of his correspondences with Mr. Brian Fritz, of the Somerset County Archaeology Society, which help provided some understanding of the stone. Tom confirmed that there is no date engraved on the stone, unlike the Christian Cross Stone located nearby. Since the Mountain family is believed to have carved the Christian Cross Stone, Tom believes that if they too carved the Sentinel, it would have probably been dated as well.

Brian Fritz indicated that he believed that Native Americans did not wear headdresses until the late 19th century, and that the stone graving is not likely earlier than that. However, Tom has developed evidence suggesting that some Native Americans wore feathered headdresses – not full ones – but with some feathers, as early as the 18th century. Therefore, his research would suggest that the stone could have been carved quite early. Tom suspects that the carving could go back to as early as 1750. But, who carved it, and why it was carved is unclear. Sam Bowers told me that he had heard it may have been carved by an early settler to warn travelers of possible Indian contact in the area. Franklin Ellis, who provided a considerable wealth of history regarding Fayette County, recorded nothing about the stone when he compiled records in 1882. The mystery surrounding its purpose, and artist, will probably never be discovered.

Returning to our packs, Moocher and I loaded up, and crossed Jim Mountain Road, resuming our trek. Within minutes we found another historical place: The Unnamed Cemetery. This graveyard is visible from the trail, just a short distance after crossing the highway. Every time that I hike this section, I respectfully pause at the site.

There are about 15 headstones speckling the small plot. A low, fieldstone fence surrounds it. Four of the headstones are common fieldstones. Only three head stones are yet legible. These three mark the final resting place of Adam Dietz who died 6/08/1852, at the age of 54 years, Elizabeth, daughter of Adam & Elizabeth Dietz who died 9/08/1818 at the age of 12 years, and Mary Leonard who died 1/05/1894 at age 49. In his historical account of Springfield, Franklin Ellis mentions that one Adam Dietz was known to operate a barn for the drovers who moved livestock over Clay Pike Road. It is quite possible that the Adam Dietz buried in this plot, is the same one mentioned by Ellis.

Each time that I pause at the cemetery, I think of little Elizabeth Dietz. From an earlier journal I found these thoughts and queries that I once recorded:

> *One can't but think of little Elizabeth who lived only twelve years before coming to this shaded lot. Had she been a sickly girl? Or did the ruggedness of settler life require too much from her?*
>
> *With sweat streaming down my face, I thought of those who mourned in salty tears standing right where I stood. Were they comforted in their weeping with the words of Rev 21:4 'And He shall wipe away every tear from their eyes; and there shall no longer be any death; there shall no longer be any morning, or crying, or pain?'*

Moocher and I spent a little time near the cemetery, and then quietly moved north. By midmorning we reached a scenic formation known as Bear Rocks. This offers a very wonderful view of Middle Fork, just beyond milepost twenty-one. It is one of the nicest overlooks on the Laurel Highlands Hiking Trail. Although it is not a towering height like that above Victoria, its wide view of rolling hills never disappoints. Reportedly, on a clear day, one can see the U.S. Steel Building in Pittsburgh from these rocks. I cannot recall ever being able to see that far, but still the sight was enjoyable for us both on this clear day.

We lowered our packs, withdrew from them a morsel to eat, and sat down on the rocky ledges, soaking up the view. Beyond our feet we saw the gentle, sliding curves of hillsides rippling before us, like rolling ocean waves being pulsed in the midmorning breeze. What conversation we shared on the rocks would soon become lost to me, but the memory of that leisurely moment spent upon a rocky vista, like all such moments, has become deeply imbedded into my mind as a moment to savor.

It is for occasions like this that I come to the woods, and to walk upon the trail: to sit upon sun-warmed rocks, and gaze across gentle rolling, leafy hills; to walk unhurriedly, and without schedule; to forget the time of day, both in this world, and the one back home; to sit when tired; to eat when hungered, to stretch myself out upon grassy fields, or rocky, lofty peaks, and to nap at will. Oh, just to breathe the air that surrounds and cushions such places is to inject a tide of immortal pleasure into these temporal frames of flesh and bone. Pleasure so intense that at times I fear my skin will burst from the inward pressure of such delight.

We sat upon the rocks until our rest was complete. We then rose up and continued our northward peregrination. Immediately we began passing over some of the easiest hiking terrain that the Laurel Highlands Hiking Trail has to offer. Unlike the grueling hills that envelop Ohiopyle, the section between Route 653 and Seven Springs Resort flows nicely and smoothly along. On this day we had the good fortune of pleasant sunshine, a cool breeze, and an amicable temperature, which made our efforts all the more facile.

Though Moocher and I often walk in silence, I was glad for his company. We chattered over previous hikes, and discussed places that we would like to explore. The day continued to unfold in beauty, with a deepening blue sky above us, and lush green embracing our every step. It was not necessary to point out these things to one another, for they were not going unnoticed or unappreciated.

Just before the twenty-fifth milepost, the trail left Laurel Ridge State Park grounds, and entered the Blue Hole Division of Forbes State Forest. The Blue Hole Division is named after a deep hole of water fed by Blue Hole Creek. Not long after my hike I returned and drove into Forbes State Forest from nearby Scullton, and set out looking for Blue Hole. Without too much difficulty, I found the landmark situated along a dirt road in the Forbes State Forest. There, Blue Hole Creek courses down from the mountain and empties into a deep depression just beside the dirt road. After filling the hole it continues on its merry way. The water in Blue Hole was at least five feet deep on the day of my visit. It was crystal clear, but carried a strange bluish tint to it. Beneath the canopy of the tall trees that bent over the hole, the water was shielded from the sun, making it feel very cold. My uncle, E. "Skip" Cramer told me that when he was a young boy, his family would take a picnic lunch into that section of the forest, and then leap into Blue Hole for a cold swim. He said that the temperature was so cold it would take your breath away. But for him the treat of a summer swim was not hampered by the cold temperature of the blue waters.

In about a mile, Moocher and I came across a seldom-used pathway known as Pritts Distillery Road. This road separates the edge of Forbes State Forest and the beginning of the only privately owned property along the trail – the boundaries of Seven Springs Resort.

It was not until weeks after my hike that I learned something of the legend behind Pritts Distillery Road. It happened while I was visiting with my then next-door neighbor, Mr. Ed Lyons, a retired state employee. We somehow got into a conversation about Laurel Hill, and he shared with me that he grew up in its foothills, and knew the area quite well. He asked me if I was familiar with his great-grand dad, "Old Bill" Pritts, and the story behind Pritts Distillery Road. I pleaded ignorance on both counts and with a gleam in his eye, Mr. Lyons shared with me the dubious account of the legendary Bill Pritts, and the grisly murder that occurred in the once moonshine-riddled mountains of Laurel Hill.

Bill Pritts was born around 1837, and cut out a living in the mountains with his wife, "Aunt Hannah," and their nine children. Although he was known to make a living farming the fields, it was also well established among the hill folk that Bill Pritts was foremost a moonshiner. He was described as a giant of a man whose friendliness won the affections of his neighbors, and whose cunning foiled law enforcement agents for eight years. He was described as having had piercing blue eyes and a face covered with a long, gray beard from which a smoking pipe constantly protruded.

Old Bill lived in a farmhouse in Salt Lick Township of Fayette County Pennsylvania, about 100 yards from the Somerset County line. In the late 19th century, all throughout Laurel Hill, illegal moonshine stills were hidden in hollowed-out trees, beneath rocks, and atop hard-to-reach cliffs. Although Bill reportedly did not drink his own homemade liquor, he made plenty from a recipe, which ingredients he would not divulge. An unspoken oath existed among the moonshiners that one would never tattle on another. It is believed that that oath, broken by a local man, put Old Bill on a path of deadly destruction.

On the afternoon of March 30, 1892, James Beal, who

had been visiting his sister in Somerset County, was returning to his home in Westmoreland County. A light snow had fallen that morning across the mountain, but not enough to dissuade Beal from hiking over Laurel Hill. He followed a trail that led him through the village of Trent where he passed close by the Trent store, and continued without difficulty for about two more miles. As Beal approached a turn in the trail, he heard a voice crying out, "Halt!" Believing that someone was calling for him, he paused to listen, and when the command was sounded again, he took refuge in some bushes.

From his vantage point, Beal claimed to have seen three men, all armed with firearms drawn menacingly in their hands. Beal saw the three talking with a fourth man who was standing in the middle of the road. Beal heard voices, but could not determine what was being said. Suddenly, he heard the report of gunfire, and witnessed a brutal attack by the three armed men upon the fourth. Using their weapons as clubs, he saw them unmercifully beat the outnumbered man about his head and body. Beal, fearing he might be discovered as a witness, retreated back into the forest, and quickly made his way back toward Trent. On his way he stopped at the Hochstetler homestead to ask for alternate directions to his sister's house. There, he spoke with Mrs. Hochstetler, and reported what he had witnessed. Mrs. Hochstetler was waiting for her husband, John, to return home along the same path that Beal had taken, but she was not alarmed, and in fact, did not really believe Beal's story. She did not know that by that time she was already a widow.

Beal continued his way back to Trent, and reported the violent attack that he had witnessed to those gathered in the store. Several recalled that John Hochstetler had been in the store earlier that afternoon and immediately began to fear that he may have been the victim. A search party was formed with Beal leading the way. At the crime scene the disturbed snow along the path disclosed signs of a great struggle, and revealed that something heavy had been dragged off of the trail. A search of the area quickly revealed a badly mutilated body, partly submerged in a small creek that runs along what is known today as the Copper Kettle Highway. The victim was soon identified as John Hochstetler.

An investigation led to the arrest of two moonshiners, William C. Miller, and his son, Robert, both who were not unfamiliar to the magistrates, or to the interiors of their jails. It was suspected that Mr. Hochstetler may have broken the vow of silence among the moonshiners, and was considered too costly of a liability. As Robert was taken into custody, he confessed to being present during the crime, but insisted that his father and Bill Pritts had actually committed the murder. An arrest warrant was issued for Bill Pritts and thus began an eight-year cat-and-mouse game between the old mountain man, and the relentless authorities.

U.S. Marshals and local law enforcement agents began scouring the hills for Old Bill. It was during this time that Old Bill's fame grew among the locals, and his name took on legendary status with them. He knew the mountains well, and continued to elude his pursuers at every turn. Legend has it that Old Bill had a dog that could detect Bill's enemies long before they drew near, and that the canine had saved Bill from apprehension on several occasions. Bill's wife also provided stiff resistance. In 1895, Secret Service Agent, G.H. Fisher learned that Bill Pritts was in his house and as he approached to make the arrest Mrs. Pritts suddenly stormed out of with broom in hand. She struck him with such great force that he eventually abandoned the idea of making the arrest, and fled the area.

But the persistent work of law enforcement agents eventually paid off. In the spring of 1900, Fayette County Detective Alexander McBeth, and Federal Deputy Marshal W.J. Dickson, set out on what would be their final effort to apprehend Old Bill. Surveillance of Bill's house only resulted in alerting the legendary dog, and Mrs. Pritts, who both began a pursuit that chased the agents deep into the mountain. The next morning they assumed a surveillance position along a worn path that led from Old Bill's place to his son-in-law's house. Their efforts were rewarded as they observed Old Bill's youngest son walk by. They covertly followed him, and were eventually led to Pritts, who was dozing against a fence rail. The agents separated and approached Old Bill who awoke with a start. He saw Agent McBeth and turned to run, only to find himself staring down the business end of Agent Dickson's Winchester rifle. Without further incident, Old Bill was arrested and taken to the county jail in Uniontown.

By this time Old Bill had taken on legendary status with the local community, and they rallied for him by collecting bail money. According to Paul E. Fuller of the *Meyersdale Republican* even the *Connellsville News* seemed enamored by him as they reported that he had been arrested "on a trumped up charge."

Old Bill denied the murder charges, but admitted he was present when the crime was committed. Because there wasn't enough evidence to convict him, he was eventually set free with the stipulation that he had to pay the revenuers the money due for the moonshine he made. Old Bill returned to the mountains and built a distillery along Neal's Run Creek, where he legally bottled his liquor. My neighbor, Mr. Lyons, who shared this story with me, drove me one bright summer afternoon to the site where the distillery once stood, just off the Laurel Highlands Hiking Trail. A concrete retaining wall is all that remains of the building; but Neal's Run still bubbles nearby, feeding Indian Creek. A short distance from the retaining wall stands a stone monument erected by Old Bill's descendents in memory of this dubious mountain legend. Mr. Lyons also drove me to Tinkey Cemetery where we visited Bill Pritts and his wife's gravestone, which are found about one mile from where the celebrated mountain man once lived.

Moocher and I crossed Pritts Distillery Road and continued our journey north. The morning walk was going smoothly as we prattled merrily along. The wind was blowing strongly, bending the grasses and trees with its unseen hand. Though the sun was out and it was a splendid day for walking, we were encountering no one else on the trail. As the noon-hour approached, we both agreed that we were deserving of an extended break, and so we began looking for a place where we might enjoy our lunch. I was hoping for a spot in the sun, and so we passed up several choice locations in the woods, searching for that perfect resting place. Our feet eventually led us to a break in the woods where an old road passed by. Here, cushiony grass hugged the dirt road, and provided the ideal place to stretch our aching legs in peaceful comfort. Our heavy packs fell with a dull thud on the grassy strip, and tasty victuals were withdrawn from them. With no small amount of satisfaction, we enjoyed our lunch in the warm sunlight.

After eating, I slipped out of my boots and squirmed against my backpack until I had found a comfortable position. With the grass tickling the souls of my feet, I stretched my legs across the green lawn of the forest's edge. The oft-quoted words of the Psalmist, *He maketh me to lie down in green pastures,* came to my mind like a feathery pillow as I drifted in and out of sleep among the waving blades of lush grass. Moocher did not disturb me, leading me to believe that he had found his own place among the woodsy fairies that playfully dash in and out of the sleep-drenched, trail-tired mind. We welcomed the moil of slumber within our tired bones, and in the arms of Morpheus finished our labor of sleep beneath the shades of waving oaks and towering maples. Outside the world of time clocks, and deadlines and obligations, we drank freely from the fountain of drowse, returning again and again to fill our cups to the brim of unhurried rest.

When the season of repose had sufficiently passed, we began to stir. Prodding one another with conversation deficient of meaning, we slowly rose from our perfect positions, and saddled ourselves beneath our packs. Renewed both in body and spirit we returned to our northward march.

Our early afternoon walk led us atop some of the ski slopes of Seven Springs Mountain Resort, and the highest point on the trail at 2950 feet. It was here that we began to encounter other people. We first met a toddler who was securely perched atop the shoulders of his smiling father. Beside them walked a beaming woman whose perfume made us both sniff curiously at ourselves as we passed by. They said they were staying at the resort and were enjoying the sun while exploring the sloping hillsides.

We next encountered a number of bicyclists who were pedaling their way up a steep mound. It seemed they could not afford the breath to speak with us, although some acknowledged our presence with a nod or swift wave as we passed one another.

Passing by Seven Springs, Moocher and I returned to Forbes State Forest grounds. The trail turned slightly northeast, leading us briefly into Westmoreland County, and then back into Somerset County. Moocher moved ahead of me, and for a mile or so, I did not see him. Eventually I caught him as he paused to rest on one of the ascents, which we were now beginning to find with greater frequency. As we continued our walk north, Moocher again moved ahead. In a short span of time I met two hikers who were traveling south on the trail. Carrying only hydration packs on their backs, they seemed to be out for one day's journey on the trail. We greeted one another as we passed on the trail, but did not pause to talk. I met Moocher again on another ascent, and we began the climb together. It was the first challenging ascent that we experienced all day, and came as a bit of a shock to our systems. My thermometer registered 80° in the forest, and in moments, we were both soaked in our sweat. The thermal cooling affect of the wind suddenly seemed to die off as if the old mountain wanted to challenge us a bit.

I suppose in a perfect hiking world, there would only be shaded paths built along level wooded planes. These ideal trails would take one past breath-taking overlooks, uninhibited by trees or other obstacles, and provide frequent sightings of rarely seen animals. Water could be freely drunk from any streambed, and backpacks would be measured not by their weight, but by how much more comfortable they made one feel.

I reckon that it is just human nature to desire paths of least resistance. Whether we are climbing a steep hill, or facing a taxing dilemma, we often wish to be anywhere else but there. Yet, is it not resistance that builds stamina, and is not pleasure increased through our understanding of pain? I never knew what a good night's sleep was really about until I had to walk the floor with a crying baby at three in the morning. And I do not believe I could ever fully appreciate the refreshing taste of cool clear water without first having felt heat and thirst. Does it feel better to recline with one's legs raised to a footstool after a day of relaxing, or a day of testing labor? Perhaps our toils could be better endured if we would pause in them and reflect on the value they bring to our lives through richer appreciation of rest.

Moocher and I climbed the steep hills of the Laurel Highlands Hiking Trail while the silently cheering foliage applauded our passing with receptive rustles and warm waves. We paused often to catch our breath, and for inspirational purposes, turned to look back upon the incline we had just scaled. As the path rounded the top of the hill, our breathing returned to a more regular inhaling, and our legs muscles did not quiver so. A sudden but short sprinkle of rain greeted us at the top, and as if a heavenly light switch was thrown off, the sky abruptly became a darkening purple. While the sky dimmed itself, we trekked into a towering section of evergreen trees whose branches reached out to soak up any remaining light. These branches cast upon the forest floor piles of soft needles that absorbed the fall of our thick-soled hiking boots like a cushiony carpet. The air in this darkened room was filled with the perpetually burning incense of sticky pine, and the aura was that of a quiet sanctuary – one that we did not wish to disturb. We found a giant gnarled maple tree near the northern entrance of this woodsy sanctuary. A tumor-like knot extended from its rib and from a distance it appeared to have already given up the ghost. But Moocher found some green leaves shooting from its twisted branches and pointed them out to me. This faithful sentry of the sanctuary still lived, dutifully watching the forestry portal placed at its charge. As we passed by, we noted that the sky began to brighten as if the sun was returning from business done elsewhere.

Continuing our walk, we crossed Route 31, which runs precisely through the Somerset-Westmoreland County line, on the summit of Laurel Hill. Route 31 is a two-lane paved, east-west road bearing the name Glades Pike Road as it courses through Somerset County. The eastern edge of the roadway lies in Bedford County, Pennsylvania, where it joins Route 30. The western terminus is just outside of the town of West Newton in Westmoreland County, Pennsylvania. This is one of the oldest roads through Somerset County and over Laurel Hill. Long before the white man came to this section of land, the area was almost completely covered by forest. There were, however, many glades or natural meadows in the region. So frequently found were these natural openings that the area began to be referred to as "The Glades" by the white man who passed through. By most accounts the "Old Glades Pike" was believed to have originated as an Indian path. Its discovery by the Europeans, who were constantly seeking a quicker passage west, increased its popularity. Soon the path, widened for carts and wagons, began to take on the semblance of a roadway. For many years, before the Old Forbes Road and Braddock Road were completed, the Old Glades Road was the most important passage to the Ohio Valley from the East.

Stepping out from the woods, and moving north across the road, we felt the heat rising from the smoldering macadam of the heavily trafficked road. Not only was it much hotter outside of the woods, but it was much brighter too. We squinted in the brightness of the day, whose light had not been fully appreciated until now, and quickly directed our steps toward the small opening in the woods on the other side where the trail waited.

The hard road was an unwelcomed sensation beneath my boots. The soles of my feet had been aching for the past hour or so, and I was looking forward to extracting them from their leathery, Gore-Tex huts, and lifting them to a comfortable resting position well above the ground. Moocher and I were walking together when we both saw the sign that directed us off of the trail, and toward the Route 31 Shelters. Drawing nearer to the shelters we suddenly realized that we were no longer alone in this section of the woods. Friendly-sounding voices generously mixed with laughter brought news to us that others were already enjoying the crude benefits of the shelter area.

During the busy summer hiking season on the trail it is not uncommon to meet other hikers who are seeking refuge for the night at the same shelter area that you may have selected. One never knows what kind of company that one might be spending the night with on the trail. Some hikers have come to the woods to withdraw, and will characteristically remain quite taciturn throughout the night. Others seem to be struggling with the solitude that the forest has brought upon them, and nearly stumble over themselves in excessive prattle, liberally dispensing words as if ending a prolonged vow of silence. Then, of course, there is the more dubious nocturnal neighbor who always seems to spin a bit more eccentric than the rest, making one wonder what they are doing out in the woods. One encounter with a person of this nature occurred at a hostel along the Appalachian Trail in Virginia as my companions and I came to find rest there for the night. He came in very late in the day with no baggage or pack, and gave no accounting of his day or journey. His attire did not clearly suggest, or deny, that he had been hiking that day, and it was just as reasonable to guess from his polished shoes that he could have well been returning from his job as a used car salesman at some three-car lot.

He never described where he was going, or where he had been. He did not reveal his hometown, or details of his personal life that hikers are oftentimes prone to reveal in friendly, fireside exchange. He did not remain silent, however, but joined us in the middle of our detailed conversations as if he had not only been present at their inception, but had instigated and inspired them. That night it seemed that he emptied himself of every opinion he ever had, and became completely swept up in the illusion that our very lives were hinged upon his ability to talk without ceasing. Eventually we made a successful escape of the blather by crawling into our sleeping bags, and feigning sleep. However, he merely exchanged his one-sided verbal conversation for another form, as he too bedded down with us, and for the duration of the long night, disrupted our sleep with the most disturbing sound of peace-shattering flatulence. We were all relieved to be on our way as morning dawned the following day.

As Moocher and I wandered into camp that late afternoon, we soon discovered that our evening would hold promise of a pleasant one. At the first shelter that we approached we found two adult men, and several young boys. Ample provisions were spread out between two shelter lean-tos, and they were reclining on comfortable-appearing camp furniture. It became immediately apparent, based on the abundance of camping equipment, that they were not engaged in a long-distance hike on the trail. Instead, they shared with us that they were setting up camp for three teenage hikers who were hiking the 70-mile trail in just two days. Earlier that same morning they had dropped the three young adventurers off at the northern end of the trail near Seward. They then dispensed food and water supplies at pre-determined points along the trail for the young men, who were hiking with minimal provisions. The supporting group then moved to this shelter area, which was close to being a halfway point on the trail, and set up camp, awaiting the boys' arrival. We had a nice chat with the group, and then Moocher and I turned our attention to making our own camp for the night.

Our lean-to was situated across a small stream, and away from the center of the shelter area. We made our way to the crude shelter, and dropped our packs on the hard wooden floor before carefully lowering ourselves down to rest. There are few sensations that can best the feeling of being relieved of a backpack after a long day's journey. Fourteen miles of twisting trail had depleted from our veins the moxie that just this morning had bubbled within us most liberally.

We entirely relaxed ourselves, and did not interrupt those first few minutes of sacred rest with senseless activity or needless conversation. Instead, we sat motionless, trying to sop from the paint-faded planked floors of the shelter, any energy that might have been left behind by its previous visitor. At the same time we were cognizant of the need to ambulate before the crucial moment when rest is overtaken by immovable muscle stiffness - which can easily ruin any vestige of rest that leisure had labored to deposit.

Finally we stirred and began to make our camp. We discussed building a fire. But, noting that the firewood pile was located down across the stream, and up beyond the other bank, we decided against it. We made several trips to the hand pump and replenished our scant water supply, while collecting enough for our evening meal. From my fossil-fueled camp stove, we made our supper, and then had our postprandial mug of instant hot chocolate while focusing more intently upon relaxing.

Some time around nine o'clock in the evening, the three young endurance hikers came into camp. Moocher and I were already tucked into our sleeping bags, but could hear them being greeted warmly by their waiting comrades. The boys made their way to the shelter closest to Moocher and me and prepared for their night of rest. We overheard them complaining of tired muscles and sore feet, but having just hiked over thirty-seven miles, I felt that they were still bounding with considerable energy. One of the young men had rigged up a speaker system into his backpack, and was playing CDs as they hiked. However, this was causing them some inconvenience – not because of the extra weight – but because they were going so fast down some of the hills that the CD player would skip, and their musical entertainment was being interrupted.

The carefree nuances of their raillery brought to mind my own days of youthful romp, when fun with friends was not only one of life's greatest rewards, but at times its sole focus. As Moocher stirred on his mat, trying to find the position offering the least discomfort, my mind was rocketed back to a crisp autumn night when he and I would meet under less tranquil circumstances. Not only is Moocher one of my hiking companions, but he is my uncle, and for a few years, was the leader of the youth group that I belonged to at church. In our teen years, Halloween brought a special time for my friends and me. We cared naught for the costumes and treats of the holiday, but sought only the "tricks" that we enjoyed playing in our neighborhood. Soaping windows and toilet-papering homes became an adventure whose lure far outweighed the consequences of what we believed was improbable capture. We did not randomly hit local homes, but selected only the ones belonging to people who we believed could take a joke.

On one particular night we decided to venture out and visit a few of our favorite homes. Moocher's house was on our list but we knew it would not be easy. He was quite aware of how the season cultivated our capricious natures, and, having personally performed the very same kinds of pranks not too many years before, Moocher had a good idea of when and how we would be striking.

We decided that it would be too risky to park on Moocher's street and try approaching his house. We knew he would be looking for us and would be startled by any strange car stopping nearby. So, we concocted another plan: we would do a slow drive-by, while my younger brother, Kyle, slipped out. He would approach the house and soap a few windows, while we drove around town. We would return in a few minutes and spirit him away before anyone was the wiser.

We passed Moocher's house and saw the interior lights turned on. This would be an added bonus. Soaping someone's windows while the family was asleep offered only limited rewards. But soaping a home's picture window while the family was watching TV would be something to boast about. Indeed, a daring raid like this would most certainly give birth to legend – if not inspire at least a few folk songs about us.

Our friend was driving and I was sitting in the back seat. We eased up near Moocher's home and Kyle slipped out before we ever came to a complete stop. Under cover of darkness, he hoped to make his way to the windows of the house and leave his soapy calling card, while we inconspicuously left the neighborhood. But as he began creeping across the yard, he saw movement near Moocher's house. Freezing motionlessly behind a tree he slowly peeked around. As his eyes adjusted to the darkness, he saw Moocher already outside. Apparently our slow drive-bys had alerted Moocher to trouble, and he had moved outside to set up a protective perimeter about his domicile.

The tense moments ticked by for Kyle, but eventually he realized that he had not been seen. Moocher was hiding behind one tree, while Kyle hid behind another, not twenty feet apart. We circled slowly around town giving plenty of time for a good soaping, totally unaware of the tense drama unfolding in Moocher's yard. Finally, we returned to the scene. Our plan was to roll slowly past, pick up Kyle, and then make a quick and triumphant getaway.

We came down Moocher's dead-end street, and turned around at the end. Slowly approaching his house again we could see Kyle standing in the yard, behind a tree. None of us in the car suspected that another figure lurked in the blackness of the night, watching our every move. As we approached, we saw Kyle standing quite still, making no effort to make his getaway. Finally, we stopped the car and began to call out in whispered shouts for him to hurry before the occupants of the victim's house were roused by the unusual disturbance on an otherwise quiet street.

Kyle glanced back at Moocher who was still unaware of his presence, and then at us in the car, trying to figure out a way to escape from his desperate predicament. Surprise, coupled with whatever speed he could muster, would be his only hope. So, in a sudden blinding flash, he left the safety of the tree's protection, and sprinted towards the waiting vehicle. At nearly the same time, to the surprise of everyone in the car, Moocher broke free from the shadows of another tree, and the race was on while we could only helplessly watch.

Kyle raced towards the car, and, not having time to enter conventionally, dove headfirst through the open window, while at the same time screaming, "Get out of here!" The driver slammed heavily on the throttle while Kyle was still making his unusual entrance. Moocher had reached the car a fraction of a second later, and had time to seize Kyle's feet, which were dangling out of the window, having not yet ceased from their sprinting motion. From the relative safety of the back seat I had the privilege of witnessing the not-too-oft seen tug-of-war, between a tire-spinning, gravel-kicking Olds 88, and a house-and-home-defending champion, while a human rope was suspended betwixt.

We made our escape that night, having successfully retrieved Kyle from the clutches of Moocher, only to tell and re-tell the story many times. It never grew old in recounting, nor did it waiver in adventuresome lure. Eventually, it became one of those stories that pile atop the others, marking us, and making us, who we are today. We all have stories like that. Often they do not contain any great moral significance or meaning. They are just stories that bring together friends, family and good times. We keep them safely tucked away and whenever we need a smile, we simply reach into the rain barrel of memories and take out what we need.

Moocher and I listened to the boys chat well into the evening. Eventually, however, every one of us succumbed to the heavy dose of slumber's unavoidable drip, and the night became another mark in the endless line of nights that await each day's end.

Day Four

I t was our young neighbors in the next door shelter who first broke the membrane of sleep. The day had already been brimming in dawning glory when they began emerging from their sleeping bags. Their restless stirring sent a jarring fissure across my comatose state and my eyes soon began taking in their first glimpses of morning light.

Slowly I raised myself to a seated position while still partially in my sleeping bag. It took a few moments to acclimate myself to the sensation of consciousness. Looking around, I began to recognize certain items that mutely reminded me that I was not at home in bed atop soft clean sheets. Like a faithful steed my backpack hung patiently at the shelter entrance waiting for me to saddle myself into it and take it to the woods where it could freely roam. Above me on the lean-to's small plank shelf were my cooking utensils and stove, still neatly lined together ready to be filled and fired for a hot breakfast. These sights silently greeted me with the sobering reality that there was much to do and many miles to walk today.

Crawling out of my sleeping bag I happened to glance down to the shelter floor. Not far from where my head had been lying, I saw the telltale sign of some nocturnal visitors. Like tiny pieces of dirt, mouse droppings were scattered across the wood floor. Apparently we had unknowingly entertained visitors during the night.

I am not particularly fond of the constituents of the murine kingdom, and so I simply refused to think about all of the places that the rodents might have scurried while we slept. I was just thankful that I learned of their visit *after* they had vacated our shelter. Otherwise it would have been a very, very long night for me.

My uneasiness about mice is not wholly unwarranted. On June 28, 1993 a 61-year-old man was admitted to a southern Pennsylvania hospital. He was in acute respiratory distress, and had a four-day history of fever, chills, diarrhea, and vomiting. His mysterious condition initially worsened, but then eventually began to respond to treatment. He remained in the hospital for nearly a month.

The man reported that in April of that year he had started hiking the Appalachian Trail in Georgia. He walked through Georgia, North Carolina, Tennessee, and spent the few preceding weeks in Virginia.

Just prior to this man's illness, a similar outbreak was occurring in the "Four Corners" area of the country: Colorado, New Mexico, Arizona, and Utah. There, a young healthy Navajo man was on his way to his fiancée's funeral when he experienced shortness of breath. He was rushed to the hospital but died very rapidly. His fiancée had died of the same symptoms. A review of the recent deaths revealed that five healthy people had died of the same symptoms in the past few weeks.

An intensive investigation was launched by the Center for Disease Control. It was discovered that the Four Corners area had experienced unusually heavy spring rains, producing a bumper crop of mice. A common thread was found in the history of the 61-year-old Appalachian Trail hiker who reported seeing evidence of mice in the many lean-tos and bunkhouses that he slept in just prior to becoming sick.

The mysterious illness was eventually identified as *Hantavirus*. It is a virus carried by rodents, mainly the deer mouse, contained in their urine, droppings, and saliva. People contract the disease by breathing air contaminated by the virus. A serious condition, it had proved fatal in nearly half of the cases initially identified. By 2005 the CDC reported 384 diagnosed cases. Over one third of those died from the virus.

Although very few cases of *Hantavirus* were diagnosed in Pennsylvania, that fact contributes nothing towards the affection I feel for mice.

One of the young boys from the shelter next door was still in his sleeping bag. The night must not have been as kind to him, as his companions, as I heard him beg, with sleep still heavy in his eyes, "Please, don't ever think of doing this again."

After Moocher and I had breakfast, we packed our belongings. He would be turning around and hiking back to Route 31 where his wife would pick him up. I would continue my northbound hike. The boys were heading south with hopes of reaching Ohiopyle by nightfall. They were still preparing for their long hike as we left camp. We wished them Godspeed as we walked past their shelter. Weeks later I would learn via email that by twilight they reached their objective. They were sore, blistered and tired, but they had realized their objective of having put away seventy miles in two days.

Moocher and I walked to the Laurel Highlands Hiking Trail. He turned south and I turned north. Immediately, as I moved ahead alone, I sensed how much I had been enjoying the presence of someone else. This sensation came as no real surprise. I believe that there are very few people who are genuinely solitary folk. We may enjoy our time alone, and even accomplish many great things while isolated, but I do not believe that we were created to continually and optimally function that way. The ventures that we succeed at while we are alone are significantly enhanced when we share them with others. For me, being alone is a discipline that sharpens my communal awareness, and sends me back better equipped to remain a social being.

The morning sun hung low in the sky, and, unimpeded by clouds, rained its great rays of light down across the dewy forest. Silently, the green leaves, ferns and grasses busied themselves with the photosynthetic process of transforming the sunlight into the energy needed to grow, and into the carbohydrates that the plant-eating animals were dependent upon to live; who in turn would become the protein that the carnivores of the forest stalked.

It is a splendid and delicate system. Yet, in spite of the magnificent design of the ecological system, it pales in comparison to the design and value of one single species; the sometimes notorious, occasionally meritorious, indubitably vainglorious genus, whose ambassador this author and his readers are – the firmly-established *Homo sapiens*.

However, it is not with our accomplishments that we have induced our worth. Nay, I reckon that if all the great deeds of humanity were measured against our transgressions and failures, we would still fall pitifully short of any mark of significance.

Our unquestionable value, then, cannot come from the strides of humane doctrine or practice that we pride ourselves with from time to time. Instead, it is delivered by a heredity that we must humbly recognize as originating from outside of ourselves. It began with a single breath; yet not a breath that even our lungs could boast of inaugurating. For it was a breath blown *into* our lungs – not outward – that caused this worth to begin its wash within our veins. Being fashioned by our Creator only humankind can claim to be the recipient of God's breath, the Breath of Life, blown into our nostrils.

This is what separates us from all of creation; not the opposable thumb that allows us to grasp; not the reasoning process that allows us to build and fashion; nor even is it our ability to experience love that propels us to this higher plane. No, it is our breath. The breath that God first blew into us has left upon us the unmistakable thumbprint of a loving Creator. This breath, moving in and out of our lungs, sets us apart, and brings to our lives the value and worth that we all possess. And with each breath we take we testify to the worth found in us.

My breathing was deep this morning. Several small, steep hills were lying in wait for me just north of camp. I set them behind with a coffee-induced vigor, and then continued moving northward at a casual pace.

The weight of my pack felt good, nestled snuggly on my back. My trekking poles – ski poles for hiking – were in my hands, swinging ahead of me in even syncopation, finding sure ground and assisting in the bearing of my load. Feeling good, and being surrounded by goodness, it was most certainly a good day to be walking.

With one eye on the trail before me, searching for even footing, I tried to keep another eye on the scenic forest as it leisurely rolled past. Occasionally I would pause in my walking, and linger where the forest held unusual aesthetic appeal, or to see if I might make a sighting of an animal rarely seen. Then, I would press forward only to pause again and repeat the process.

Unusual sighting or no, there is still always much to

see. And there is also much to ponder. As a matter of truth pondering becomes as natural as any other thing to do in the woods. The entire forest seems as suited to pondering as a polished oak desk does to a quiet library.

I do not believe that I would be betraying anyone's hard-kept secret when I say that many hunters escape to the woods not just to find game. Rather, many come to spend some time meditating. Oh, they will rarely call it meditation, donned in their green camouflage or fluorescent orange; but that is precisely what it is. A walk in the woods provides the tranquility for anyone to consider the things that need to be considered. The distractions offered by the forest spark the imagination, and allow a deepening focus to emerge. Even to the non-religious, and those unfamiliar with church settings, prayers can seem natural when whispered out in the wild.

In a short while, my trekking led me past a small, one-room cabin, just east of the trail. During the winter there is heavy traffic on the cross-country ski trails that pass through this area. This small cabin is used as a warming station for the skiers who are looking for a place of rest or to escape from the bitter cold that can ravage these hills.

I decided to pause for a quick inspection of the now vacant facilities. Sliding back the single bolt that secures the hut, I pushed open the creaking door and stepped into the rustic lodge. The light from the windows provided plenteous illumination, revealing two large picnic tables, a wood burning stove, and a large stack of split firewood.

On one of the tables was a student's paper notebook. It served as the cabin's register. I flipped through the pages, reading the various entries scrawled across the clean white pages. The handwriting was as unique as every author who paused to scribble a note. One person recorded a bear-sighting just outside the cabin, another wrote about finding a snake in the woodpile during a summer visit.

As the timeline of the register moved through the cold months, the hikers became skiers, who would stop by and leave record of their passing as well. It became easy to imagine the room full of warmly bundled skiers, laughing and joking with one another, telling tales of powdery trails, while stoking ever higher the warm fire inside the old iron stove.

I scribbled my name on the notebook to mark my fleeting visit and then closed its cover. I glanced once more about the quiet room and stepped outside. Closing the door behind me, I slid shut the metal bolt and returned to the trail.

Just before mid-morning I moved around a nondescript turn in the trail and came upon the thirty-five mile marker. This post marks the halfway point of the trail. I paused for a few moments at the milestone and pondered its significance. Thirty-five miles lay spent behind me; thirty-five miles lay challengingly before me. The cost of the essay had left me weary, thirsty and hungry. My body was chaffed, riddled with insect bites, and aching, while the soles of my feet felt aflame. These conditions would not dim over the second half of my voyage. But what adventure is ever taken without discomfort? What joyful end is reached without cost? I am learning that to shrink back from any noble task because of the distresses it brings denies the real pleasures of life.

Until having reached this halfway point, the accumulative steps that I had taken were always less in number than the steps that I must take. Once I stepped beyond the marker, the scales would begin tipping in the opposite direction. The steps left behind would increasingly greater than what lies ahead. I wondered if that revelation would affect the way I walked. Would I hurry the walk knowing the end was drawing near, or would I slow down and savor what remained?

I then wondered how it would impact our lives if we knew when it was that we stood just past our midway stone – when the days before us were fewer than the days behind. Would we live differently having moved past that mile marker? Would we plow along in bitterness and regret, destroying the pleasure of the walk still before us, or would we march forward, eyes wide-open seeking adventure and absorbing all the trail has to offer? Would a pessimistic outlook reduce the quality of remaining steps? Would a walk filled with wonder multiply the joy of the journey?

Moving past the mile marker I walked slightly north, and, around a very sharp bend in the trail. There, I came upon a sight that has surprised and entertained hikers for years. Pressed against the natural backdrop of trees, ferns, and rocks, is erected a steel mailbox. Attached to a metal post, the mailbox stands out in the woods in an amusingly awkward way. Generally, a notebook is kept inside the mailbox so that hikers can journal a few thoughts as they pass by. Stationed beside a great boulder, the mailbox has silently stood by the trail for years.

The mysterious origins of the mailbox were not easy to unravel. After my hike, I began to make inquiries as to the person or persons behind the out-of-place box. Those I spoke with had passed the mailbox for years but had no understanding of its origin, or to what end the old journals enjoyed.

After casually mentioning the mailbox to a cousin who was familiar with the trail, I came home one Thursday evening to find an unexpected message on my answering machine – with a name and number. With haste, I dialed the local number. The call was answered by a young man, and that same night I drove through a summer thunderstorm to the area known as Kuhntown, in Somerset County, to visit Levi Foust. When I met Levi he was just twenty-four years old. A thin man with an athletic build, Levi flashed many quiet, bashful smiles, and proved to be a great source of help.

In June of 1992, when he was eleven years old, Levi fashioned a box out of particleboard, and, following Kuhntown Road, walked to the trail's crossing. Wandering back the trail, he found a level spot and nailed the box to a tree with a small handwritten note. Written crudely with pencil, and bearing misspellings, the note reflected the innocence of his youth.

Levi wanted to know who was walking through the woods so close to his home, and he wanted to make them feel welcome as they strolled by. Initially, he left a small paper card allowing those passing by to record just their names and the date. Levi checked the box frequently and soon the hikers were leaving behind small notes.

In May of 1993, one hiker left a note suggesting that a notepad be left in lieu of a paper card, and that the box be moved about 200 yards south to a boulder that was a popular resting place. Young Levi took the advice. He removed the wooden contraption and installed a metal mailbox near the boulder. He began leaving small notepads for hikers. Those who passed by took advantage of the natural resting spot and began leaving notes that spoke of their adventures on the trail.

When I first spoke with Levi, he told me that he still had all of the notes that were left behind over the years. He told me that I could see them if I pleased. As I visited with him in his basement, I watched him descend the steps with a stack of limply hanging notebooks, faded tablets and scattered, loose-leaf papers in his arms. He placed them down in front of me and for a moment, I had the sense that

I was looking at an ancient manuscript. To decode its hieroglyphics would be to unlock trail adventures from years past.

I took the parchments home and began pouring over them. From the faded pages, between the lead pencil markings and ink scribbles came gushing an overwhelming fever of excitement. Many of the backpackers, hunters, joggers, walkers, and hikers, who had strolled by the mailbox over the years, paused to record their thoughts and now they were mine to enjoy.

Boy and Girl Scout Troops, summer camp groups, church youth parties, and gaggles of friends rested at the boulder, taking their turn with pen and paper. They reported sightings of deer, chipmunks, hawks, bears, rattlesnakes, coyotes, bobcats and even the occasional Yeti. Hikers complained of sore feet, parched throats, steep hills and poor companionship. They bemoaned tired legs, sore backs and fainting hearts. The trail had made them acutely aware of their desire for cold beer, hearty steaks, comfortable chairs, and dry beds. Some paused and recorded impromptu poetry, introspective thoughts, or stanzas from hymns. Some truly talented wanderers sketched amazing pictures. Others sported their sense of humor and scribbled lighthearted, humorous entries. Some demanded that escalators be installed over the hills, tunnels bored under them, and fast food restaurants conveniently built along the trail. One hiker, disappointed in the lack of vistas suggested that all the trees be cut down.

One of Levi's favorite recordings was found scrawled on a tennis shoe in 1994. Apparently the author, known only as John, had one shoe off when he was suddenly threatened by a swarm of bees. Not having the time to recover his removed shoe he escaped by running down the trail. When he reached the mailbox he recorded his misadventure on the remaining shoe, and left it behind, apparently having a second pair readily available. A week later two hikers found the tennis shoe that was left along the trail. They wrote a note on the side of it and placed it into the mailbox with its companion shoe. Not being able to track down the owner of the shoes, Levi transcribed the notes for posterity's sake and discarded the shoes.

Though some entries over the years were of bitter complaints ferreted from the harsh conditions, or poor planning, the general feel was one of exuberant joy or inward reflection. On the same trail people were taking different journeys. Many stopped to share something of what they were experiencing. Their scrawlings and drawings left a legacy of excitement, romance and adventure.

On the day of my thru-hike I paused at the mailbox but found no notepad inside. Levi's busy schedule had kept him away from maintaining the trail registry. Later, with Levi's approval, I would return and leave behind a notepad and pencil in the mailbox, anxious to begin reading the entries of those passing by. But, on this day, with no place to record my tour of the woods, I closed the box and continued walking.

Less than one mile north of the mailbox the trail crosses a narrow, unnatural opening where low-slung power lines pass over the hillside. One can traverse the obscure gap in a matter of seconds, and probably most who pass by would not pause; there simply is not much to see. But, it is what it *not* seen that makes the cut remarkable.

Deep within the hillside, beneath the rock-strewn corridor lies, a notable, man-made feature: the old Laurel Hill Turnpike Tunnel. This tunnel, and the Pennsylvania Turnpike, share their origins in the bitter rivalry and jealous anger of the great railroad kings of late 19th century.

During the 1800s, railroading contributed more to this country's growth than any other means of transportation. Providing freight and passenger service, railroading truly brought our coastal shores a little closer together. Railroading was a profitable business and soon its coffers swelled with great profit. Competition for railroad territory was fierce, and the fervor for its business sparked heated railroading wars.

Fueled by anger that George B. Roberts of the Pennsylvania Railroad was gaining control of traffic on the west shore of the Hudson River, William H. Vanderbilt, of New York Central & Hudson River Railroad, retaliated by invading Roberts own territory in Pennsylvania. Using a previously surveyed route between Harrisburg and Pittsburgh, Vanderbilt made plans to build the Southern Pennsylvania Railroad – "The Pennsy" – across southern Pennsylvania to compete with Roberts' railroad in the north.

In 1884, thousands of workers – many of them immigrants – poured into the hills of Pennsylvania. They cut, blasted, and dug their way across the Commonwealth. Nine tunnels were planned: one being the tunnel that would pass beneath Laurel Hill Mountain.

On January 18, 1884, workers began boring from both the east and west sides of Laurel Hill towards one another. They excavated through 813 feet of solid rock when, almost as suddenly as the work began, it ceased. On September 12, 1885, after a truce between Roberts and Vanderbilt was called, the Southern Pennsylvania Railroad project was completely abandoned. Some of the tunnels were so close to completion that the workers claimed they could hear the sounds of their counterparts through the rock between them. Yet, they would be denied the pleasure of seeing the completion of their labor. In some areas, workers were stopped so suddenly that they left their tools where they lay.

For nearly fifty years, the abandoned Southern Pennsylvania Railroad remained untouched. Vegetation reclaimed the right-of-ways, and water filled the empty tunnel systems. The mountains became quiet again.

During the mid-1930s, as the automobile's popularity was rising, an idea for a statewide highway was born. Unlike other roads, this highway would be drivable in any weather condition. It would be America's first Superhighway – the Pennsylvania Turnpike.

Planners remembered Vanderbilt's old roadbeds and tunnels, and began working to convert them into a drivable highway. Workers returned to the wild mountains and flowery meadows of Pennsylvania to continue the task of clearing the passageway. The ground beneath Laurel Hill shook once again as workers began drilling and blasting their way through the belly of the mountain. Construction went round-the-clock as crews took turns drilling, blasting and removing rubble. The work proved to be as dangerous as it was relentless when four men lost their lives in a cave-in. In addition to the tunnel at Laurel Hill, six other mountains were pierced through as the new highway began to take shape.

Finally, at one minute after midnight, on October 1, 1940, the tollbooths from Carlisle to Irwin were opened. Travelers – some who had been waiting in line for hours to be the first on the highway – began to creep across the smooth surface of the Pennsylvania Turnpike. The first driver to enter the Turnpike at the eastern terminus in Carlisle was Homer D. Romberg who made a 47-mile night ride to Fort Littleton. At the western end in Irwin, driver Carl A. Boe was not only the first to enter the Turnpike from that terminal, but he became the first to pick up hitchhikers when he was flagged down by pedestrians Frank Lorey and Dick Gangle. Holding the dubious honor of the Turnpike's first fatality is a 66-year-old man from Bethlehem, Pennsylvania, who within three weeks of the Turnpike's opening, lost control on an icy road and crashed into a bridge near Donegal.

Traffic volume on the Turnpike soon surpassed everyone's expectations. The tunnels, allowing only one lane of traffic in either direction, soon caused traffic jams that extended for miles. Eventually a decision was made to bypass Laurel Hill Tunnel, and in October 1964, the Laurel Hill By-Pass, which detours around the tunnel, was opened. The tunnel is now closed to all public traffic and a hefty fine is assessed to those who are caught conducting an unapproved inspection.

I ride the Pennsylvania Turnpike frequently. Though it seems construction crews are forever impeding its flow with their ceaseless improvement projects, the highway still offers quick east-west travel in lower Pennsylvania. One of my fondest memories of traveling the Turnpike took place on a warm spring evening.

I was driving home in my vehicle, heading east on The Pike with my mother and a friend. Traffic was moderately heavy but moving at a steady pace. As we approached the Donegal interchange, I briefly entertained thoughts of exiting and taking the last leg of our journey over the mountain on Route 31. But I felt my fine driving had propelled us into the stratum that male drivers often aspire to reach – we were making "good time." So, I chose to remain in the stream of steady traffic heading east on the Turnpike.

We traveled about two miles past the Donegal interchange when we saw brake lights simultaneously brightening the respective tail ends of the vehicles in front of us. When traffic ground to a halt, we saw black smoke billowing across the highway and upward ahead of us. Not immediately known to us, an eastbound tractor-trailer had caught fire and was burning so fiercely that it had literally melted itself to the pavement of the road. The flames and smoke made it too dangerous to pass. Very quickly the two lanes of swiftly moving cars and trucks became a parking lot of stranded motorists.

At first, we believed that whatever obstructed our passage would soon be cleared and we would be again making our way. But as the minutes ticked by and we saw the arrival of several fire department tankers, we realized that we should make ourselves as comfortable as possible, and wait out the inconvenience with as much optimism as we could muster. A number of motorists climbed from their parked vehicles and sought for vantage points from where they might catch a glimpse of the accident scene. Others waited with radios playing, trying to catch a news report describing the hold up.

After the first two hours of waiting fell behind us, and the sun dropped below the horizon, I decided to wander from my van and see what I could see. The blue sky was turning a marvelous orange in the setting sun, creating a spectacular backdrop to what proved to be a most interesting evening.

Travelers were found congregating near their vehicles, while some marched forward to investigate the accident scene at the beginning of the column. While the deep blue sky turned darker and the midnight hour approached, the flicker of the fireflies darting among the parade of parked vehicles intermingled with the stream of people wandering to and fro along the highway. Though some people were still patiently waiting in their cars reading, talking or even sleeping, others were out forming small social groups.

Surprisingly the mood of most people seemed to be upbeat. Walking back through the line of traffic, I encountered a group of young men who had set out a picnic cooler in the middle of the highway. They were gathered around it on lawn chairs, toasting the misfortune that had provided them with a reason to become festive. I met up with a cheery 43-year-old divorced mother who had thrown a shawl over her shoulders and stepped out of her small truck for a walk. She shared with me that she was driving to Philadelphia to visit an old friend on the morrow. She seemed in no way annoyed by the long wait but was marveling at the beautiful night sky from which beneath so many strangers were suddenly and unexpectedly brought together.

Parked next to me was a young couple who was on their way to vacation in northern Virginia. The man did not speak to me but only lay slumped over the steering wheel apparently trying to get some sleep in preparation of the long drive that still awaited them. The young girl at the passenger's window was friendly and every time I passed by she rolled down her window and asked if I had heard any news of progress. She told me they had traveled only an hour before being halted by the accident. She smiled, shrugged and summed up their bad luck with a chirpy, "Oh well!"

Moving among the stranded passengers, I met a man from neighboring Bedford County. He had eyed a construction pay loader doing construction work along the Turnpike and I heard him mumbling aloud what progress he could accomplish for the traffic jam if he were behind the wheel of the machine. A retired Air Force airman, who was offering bottled water to anyone who needed, ran his car battery down listening to the radio and needed a jump. He was helped by the man from Bedford County - who I saw gesturing several times in the direction of the yellow pay loader.

Several of us approached a minivan to check on an elderly couple who were patiently waiting inside. They told us they were doing fine, and even laughed over the mixed reports of rescue efforts that trickled back the line of cars.

One woman dressed in a pink sweat suit, walked swiftly by looking as though she was power walking through an upscale neighborhood. Teenagers walked by in groups laughing like they were at their favorite family campsite, and parents strolled up and down the road holding their children's hands like they were at the beach.

On that starlit night the two and half miles of highway running east of the Donegal exchange became a busy neighborhood of people throwing a very impromptu block party. There were probably a thousand stories in that line of traffic, and for a few hours those stories were twined together forming a loose but memorable knot. The spirits of most who ventured to the roadside meetings were high. For hours we talked, joked and came up with our own list of methods for moving the line of traffic. Though the night air grew chilly, we were warmed by the camaraderie that was enjoyed at the center and sides of the Pennsylvania Turnpike.

Finally, just before one o'clock am, after five hours of waiting, we saw the line of traffic beginning to move. We waved our good-byes, wished one another well, and returned to our waiting vehicles to join the great exodus that led us toward Laurel Hill. For me, the few hours spent there was a minor inconvenience in comparison to the fine memories that I collected on the concrete path.

As I hiked across the power line gap in the forest, above the old Turnpike tunnel, I reentered the forest and continued my northbound hike. I could hear the hum of cars and the distinctive rumble of tractor-trailer trucks as I walked ever closer to America's First Superhighway. The trail leveled nicely, made one final dip and then spat me out of the woods at the bank of the Turnpike. Breaking free from the quiet, shaded woods, the trail moved across the steel footbridge suspended above the Turnpike.

Strangely this is one of my favorite places on the trail. Strangely ... because the bridge is anything but quiet and secluded. Traffic roars at a hurried pace beneath the bridge both day and night, and it might seem like the last place anyone who has sought the gains of outdoor life to find enjoyable. Yet, I am fascinated to watch the cars, trucks, SUVs and tractor-trailers speeding up and down the road.

For a fleeting second I can often see a glimpse of the faces of some of the drivers and their passengers. Some are looking steadily ahead. Some are talking to their passengers and some are busy on their cell phones. Then there are those who glance upward and for a flash of a moment look my way. Before they disappear beneath my feet many will even send off a wave or smile. Those reactions cheer me, and I always return the salutation.

I gripped the chain link fence that encloses the bridge and watched the vehicles moving rapidly beneath my feet. I wondered about the drivers and passengers. I wondered where it was they were going, and if when they got there they would remember this brief moment when our paths crossed. I wondered also if they ever wondered about me. I wondered if they could, would they leave their horseless carriages and join me for a trip across the ridge? Or, did their own passions spur them to explore worlds that I might find foreign?

Crossing the bridge, I paused at the north end. To my left, located up the bank from the Turnpike was positioned one of the trail's most welcomed sights. It was, however, not a natural one, but one crafted by human hands. Protruding about ten feet from the ground, was a weathered wooden cross. Rocks laid at its base help support the fixture - though it had come to be listing about fifteen degrees to the southeast. It was about fifty yards west of the trail, and appeared to be erected on Turnpike right-of-way property. The cross was easily seen from the Turnpike if one was looking for it. Having been aware of its presence for years I often would stare at it as I passed it by on the Turnpike.

It was not until I met Levi that I learned who had positioned the cross on the hillside. Years before, he had gathered the wood, climbed the hill and erected the time-honored Christian symbol. For many years it had stood as a mute sentinel, fixing its gaze over the multitude of travelers who pass beneath it on the highway, and the hikers who walk beside it on the trail.

As it would be, my hike led me to the cross on the first day of the week – Sunday. The drone of traffic behind me suddenly seemed inaudible as I surveyed the cross. Leaning against the wire fence that separates the trail from the hillside where the cross has been raised, I reverently removed my ball cap, lowered my head, and offered my prayers.

It was late morning and I knew that there were still worshippers congregating in various parishes throughout the region. Though I was not present in body, I joined them in spirit and presented my worship, lifting my prayers of thanksgiving and supplication with theirs. Recalling the first stanzas of two hymns, I sang them above the roar of traffic behind me. There being no preacher's hand to shake, or choir to greet, I then returned my ball cap to its place of business and stepped away from the edge of the bridge. Within a few steps the forest swallowed me and there was no evidence left of my crude but meaningful worship service – just the weathered wooden cross leaning slightly toward the travelers speeding beneath it.

Within a few years of my thru-hike, I was traveling on the Turnpike one afternoon. As always I glanced up the hill to get a glimpse of the cross. Much to my surprise it was no longer visible. Suspecting that it may have fallen, I contacted Week Knees and asked him to join me on a reconnaissance trip. We scaled the steep hill to find that the cross had not fallen as suspected, but had clearly been cut down with a saw. It was sectioned in logs that were scattered coldly about. Although I am not certain, I suspect that the Turnpike folks may have had something to do with it since it is on their property. I was very saddened to see it go.

Reentering the woods, I found the trail beginning to twist and turn much more abruptly than before. It also moved over numerous small streambeds. These can be swollen with water when the spring rains melt winter's white mark upon these altitudinous hills. As I marched forward, the noise of rubber tires rolling against the paved ribbon were shielded by the acoustic barrier of the trees. The exhaust fumes and other smells associated with heavy traffic were soon overwhelmed by the wild fragrances of the lush forest. The quiet singing of birds and the creaking of trees replaced the man-made noises.

As I walked, I became increasingly aware of my body's growing demand for nourishment. I considered stopping to eat but could not decide on a proper location. Finding a place to eat in the woods is not always a simple task. Logs and stones can sometimes make suitable chairs, but they are not always found in the most desirable places.

Choosing a dining setting in the woods with the correct ambience is just as important as selecting a proper table in a fine restaurant. For example, a hard rock with a view is always better than a moss-covered log in the thicket. For, eating is much more than a necessity; it is a rite.

And so as I walked along the trail, I kept an eye out for a good place to relax and enjoy my noontime meal. However, as I walked along, I could not find an agreeable place, and so I decided to hold off on lunch until I reached scenic Beam's Rock.

As I treaded northward, I noted a marked difference in the trail. It was much narrower than south of the Turnpike Bridge, and the grass seemed higher, reaching out to tickle my bare legs as I walked by. The Laurel Ridge State Park office provides maintenance for the trail from Ohiopyle to the Turnpike Bridge. From the Bridge to the northern end of the trail, Linn Run State Park controls maintenance.

I continued to walk, mostly keeping my eyes on the ground before me so that I could warn my boots of any place that they should not tread. But occasionally my eyes would drift upward and seize glimpses of the forest that moved slowly along, always matching my pace or refraining whenever I paused.

There were trees to see, which in the late morning wind, swayed in gentle circles like painter's brushes against a ready canvas. The forest's understory waved in cheery animation. Lying beneath them were the logs. They were covered with moss, and in varying stages of decay. They stretched themselves randomly across the forest floor and into comfortable resting places that would last them unto their resurrections. And there were always stones to see. Some were boulders that I passed around. Others were small pebbles that were kicked up by my boots. Always there is something to see to any who chose to look.

What I did not see, however, was an ever-darkening sky. The thickly leafed canopy had shielded my eyes from angry storm clouds that had been silently gathering just atop the mountain. My first warning of impending rain was a bone-rattling peal of thunder that nearly shook the ground beneath me. Peering up through the trees I recognized for the first time the familiar foreboding colors of a summer storm.

As with any mountain range, sudden storms are common on Laurel Hill. Air moving across the flatlands reaches the foot of the mountain, and having no place to go, is pushed up the side of the hill only to meet currents of different temperatures. Whenever warm air meets cold, precipitation results.

There was simply no preparing for this storm. It did not precede itself with light sprinkles or swirling gusts of wind, but came upon the forest with a hostile viciousness – as though a gigantic bladder in the sky had been stretched beyond its limits and suddenly burst forth its contents.

The cold, pounding rain literally took my breath away. It was like I had jumped into a swimming pool without first testing its temperature with a shy toe. In a single movement, I swiftly released the sternum and belt strap that held my backpack and dropped it to the ground behind me. From one of the pack's pockets, I removed its waterproof protective cover and quickly secured it about the pack.

My sleeping bag is made of goose down. This type of stuffing keeps it light, and makes it the perfect insulation for the chilly nights on Laurel Mountain. However, it does not hold up well to water. If the goose down draws damp, my night will be most miserable.

After securing my backpack I donned my rain jacket. But it was too late. In the few minutes that it took me to cover my backpack the rain had done its damage. I was completely soaked.

I moved forward in the pouring rain. It was the kind of

cloudburst that was likely causing drivers to pull off the nearby roads to wait for a respite. But there was no place in this section of the forest to find shelter, and so I continued pressing northward.

After a few minutes in the downpour, I began to feel a strange sensation in my right boot. It felt incredibly like moisture but I refused to accept it. My boots were brand new, and were selected for their ability to remain waterproof. Yet, as I continued to walk along, I could no longer deny that water was leaking not only into my right boot, but my left as well.

What began as an irritating dampness soon became a swimming pool for my feet. With every step I could feel water squishing between my toes, and soon saw white foam bubbling out of the sides of the boot as the water was being forced out by the pumping of my foot.

The farther I walked, and felt the ponding effect of water in my boots, the angrier I became. I had purchased the boots just weeks before leaving on this hike and wore them almost everywhere to quickly break them in. Made of Gortex they were guaranteed not to leak. Yet they were filling with so much water that I thought for certain that I could fill my drinking canteen with their contents.

When the rain subsided, I decided to pause in my walk, and tend to my feet. Finding a large log, I gingerly lowered myself upon it, still strapped to my heavy backpack. Bending over, I started to undo my bootlace when I heard a nearly indiscernible noise on the trail behind me.

Startled, I looked up to see a very large hiker standing just a few feet away. It was a marvel that he had managed to move his large frame along the trail and approach so quietly. He was wearing a blue and yellow Gortex raincoat that was zipped up around his large frame. On his head he wore a Gortex safari-styled rain hat with the string strapped loosely around one of his chins. His blue nylon pants hung over muddied hiking boots. His eyeglasses were nearly steamed shut but the presence of two friendly appearing eyes could be seen behind the lenses. His lower lip jutted forward having been filled to overflowing with a rub of snuff.

"Havin' trouble, are ya?" he asked watching me unlace my boots. He was huffing rather hard though this section of the trail was relatively level.

"Yeah," I responded, "I've got some water in my boots."

My visitor's face turned serious as he watched me remove my right boot. I turned it upside down and poured the water that had been trapped inside.

"Whoa! That's alotta water!" he said with surprise. He took off his eyeglasses and, withdrawing a blue bandanna from his back pocket, began to clean the lenses for a better look at my situation.

"Yeah," I replied, "and these are brand new boots."

"You shoulda' bought boots made ah' Gortex," he said, "They don't leak at all."

"Actually, these boots *are* made of Gortex," I said as I shook the last of the water from the boot.

"Can't be," he said firmly.

"Why's that?" I asked as I pushed a handkerchief inside to absorb the excess water.

"Well, if they were made ah' Gortex they wouldn't be leakin'," he said with all seriousness.

I decided not to reply but quietly removed the two socks from my right foot. The outer sock was a soft synthetic hiking sock. It provides some cushioning and helps move moisture away from the foot. Closest to my foot I wear a silky wicking sock. In addition to moving moisture away from the foot, the soft sock protects against blisters by reducing friction.

I wrung out each sock the best that I could. For being material that typically does not absorb water they were surprisingly soaked. My new friend watched in fascination while leaning his weight forward on his walking stick. He turned away to eject some tobacco juice from his mouth so that he could speak more freely.

"You really oughta' wear hikin' socks," he said thoughtfully. "They won't hold water like those cotton ones."

"These *are* hiking socks – they aren't made of cotton," I responded wondering if he heard the mild degree of irritation in my voice.

He hadn't heard. "Can't be," he retorted. "Hikin' socks don't hold that much water."

I really was not in the mood to prove my point to this woodsy sage. Actually, I doubt that I could have proven anything to him. So, I continued trying to dry my footwear.

In silence, he watched me put my socks and boot back on. I had the sense that he had now wholly devoted himself to this project and was going to see me through it.

"Where are you heading?" I asked trying to break the awkward silence as I began working on my left boot.

"Oh, just out for a little walk." He wasn't as interested in conversation as he was in watching me work with my feet.

I was going to tell him about my own plans but it dawned on me that he had not asked and probably was not interested. So, I concentrated my energies in entertaining my new friend with my dilemma rather than distract him with cordial conversation.

Removing my left boot I turned it upside down and dumped out another surprising load of water.

"Wow! That's alotta water!" he said, evacuating some

more tobacco juice.

I nearly expressed my gratitude for his uncanny ability to narrate what was quite obvious. But instead I chose to get my feet back in working order as soon as possible and get back to some rewarding solitude.

I removed my socks from my left foot and began wringing them. The water, having been warmed by the heat inside of my boots, steamed in the steady rain. I was surprised not to hear a comment from my husky friend who was totally committed to my chore.

Finally completing my task, I put my socks back on and laced up my boots. I had considered getting dry socks from my backpack but if the boots leaked once, they could leak again. I wanted to reserve my dry socks for the evening when I could dry my gear out by a fire.

Standing up I was surprised how stiff I had become in such a short time. However, the short rest brought some of my strength back to my body, and I felt ready to move on again.

"Well, I think I'm gonna' turn around and head back now," the burly hiker said in a manner that seemed to suggest he was congratulating himself for a job well done. The look on his face made me wonder if he was waiting for me to thank him.

"Alright," I said, "I'm going to keep heading north and see how these boots hold up." I was relieved that he decided not to accompany me.

The big man unceremoniously turned around and began hiking south. I turned north and began walking. My feet felt better but I could feel some unwelcomed dampness still in my boots.

As I walked north the rain continued to fall, though it was markedly lighter. My stomach reminded me that I needed to tend to its needs, but there was no place along the trail where I might eat sheltered from the rain.

Eventually, I reached Beam's Rock where I had intended to eat lunch. This is a large outcropping of sandstone reaching upwards some sixty feet. The trail winds beneath the rocks, but there are side trails leading to the top.

Beam's Rock is most likely named after the Christopher Beam family who migrated to the area around 1793. Christopher's son, Abraham, inherited the property and was instrumental in building Beam's Church, which is located just a few miles away.

Since the rocks are easily accessible from a nearby road, it is a popular place. Hikers come out to explore the crevices and trails, while the more adventurous will repel and climb the steep cliff.

If the weather had been more favorable, I would have left the trail and circled up behind this popular vista to relax. However, the rain would have been worse in the open, and so I pushed northward.

The rain had not yet subsided and I had found no place of refuge. The need for food was nearly overwhelming, and so I stopped beyond Beam's Rock and lowered my backpack to the ground. I dug through its contents until I found my food bag. From it, I withdrew some dried beef sticks, cheese crackers, several candy bars, and a small handful of hardtack candy. I put these in my pants' pockets, and then secured the backpack over my shoulders. Lunch would be eaten while walking.

Soon afterward the rain stopped. As well as I could determine from inside the woods, the sun was revealing itself once more. In the wake of the rain, the woods took on a shiny green luster. An aroma that is distinct to the forest just after a rain permeated the air. Rejuvenated, the forest now sparkled with freshness.

During the early afternoon, I moved through a section of mature evergreen trees. So thick were their branches that it felt as though I had walked into a darkened room. I had to pause a moment and allow my eyes to adjust to the lack of light that these fathers of the forest were letting in. The floor was so thickly carpeted with pine needles that I could not even hear the sound of my walking. It was as though I was stepping inside of a sanctuary hidden from the world. The trail meandered through the room while, beside it, a tiny stream, now swollen with rain, splashed its happy welcome. Truly, this was a place where the divine meshed with the ordinary.

Not far out of the conifer sanctuary, I met a man and woman with a Golden Retriever dog who were hiking south. I saw them from a distance, and, judging from their quick pace and matching rain ponchos, recognized them as a young couple out for a day hike.

"Hello!" the woman called as we drew nearer one another.

"Hello!" I called back.

"Did you get caught in the rain?" she asked with a smile as we stopped in front of each other.

"I got soaked," I replied smiling back at her. "How about the two of you?"

"Well, we were able to get our ponchos on pretty quickly, so we didn't fare too badly," she said still smiling broadly.

I was wrong. They were not as young as I first surmised. As a matter of fact, they were decades older than I had first estimated. But it was easy to see why I was incorrect in my guess of their ages. There was a robust appearance and a vivid color about these two people – a youthful healthiness that was overwhelmingly evident. Their faces were flush with life, and a deep sparkle shone from their friendly eyes.

In addition to a plethora of other benefits, regular exercise can decelerate the affects of aging. These two strangers seemed to be walking testaments to that truth. Probably in their early sixties, they walked along with a surefootedness that suggested youthfulness, and boasted a familiarity with the out-of-doors, and of strenuous exercise.

"Where are you guys heading?" I asked.

"We're going twelve miles today – six out and six back," she replied while snapping her fingers to get their dog's attention.

The dog paid just momentary notice to her non-verbal call. Instead, it seemed entirely engrossed in the myriad of smells that the trail was surrendering to its sensitive nose. It had a beautiful golden coat suggesting a well-fed, well-tended animal. It sniffed at my boots and wagged its tail before continuing on its mysterious objective. The dog certainly seemed to be enjoying his outing.

"What about you? How far are you going?" the man asked with a smile as friendly as the woman's.

"I started in Ohiopyle four days ago, and am hoping to make it to the end in Seward in two more days," I replied.

"Wow, that's great!" the woman exclaimed with genuine excitement. "I hope you're having a good time."

"I sure am," I replied honestly.

Looking ahead, the woman saw that their dog was getting farther down the path.

"Come on, honey," she said laughingly to the man, "or we'll be left behind."

"Lead the way, sugar," he affectionately responded as they started to move around me to catch up with their dog.

I watched them go and realized that I had made another mistake in my estimation of this couple. Perhaps it was not only regular vigorous exercise, and large quantities of time spent outdoors that brought such vitality to their countenances. Maybe what gave their cheeks such a lively glow was simple and genuine affection for one another. Maybe it was a life lived in the shadow of care, cast by a figure of love that kept their youthful fires burning.

I turned north and continued hiking. My walking had generated enough body heat to begin the drying process of my clothing. However, they were still far from being depleted of moisture and were beginning to feel terribly uncomfortable.

As the afternoon passed, I continued to trudge along the trail. Suddenly I noticed that the afternoon sky was beginning to grow dark again. At first I paid little attention to the clouds, believing that they would probably change colors once more. But when a peal of thunder roared surprisingly near me, I began to pay closer attention to the rapidly changing weather indicators. I was not interested in another drenching. It would be difficult to dry my boots as they were, let alone being filled once more. So, I began to double-time my pace, hoping to cover the remaining five miles before the sky opened up again.

As I neared Route 30, the trail began to twist and bank through thick laurels. So dense were the leafy greens that visibility was reduced at times to only a few feet. With each sharp turn in the trail, my imagination began to run wild with expectations of seeing some great predator lying in wait for me. With hardly enough room to turn around, the trail offered no easy escape from an ambush. It became both thrilling and frightening to walk the path. Meanwhile the thunder continued to boom.

Nearly out of breath, I finally reached Route 30. As I stepped free from the woods I was surprised to find a light sprinkle of rain already falling. The thick foliage of the woods had shielded me, keeping me ignorant of the rain already beginning to fall.

I stood at the side of the road and watched a line of traffic move past me. Impatient drivers were crawling up the hill behind a slow-moving dumptruck filled with the contents of some mined hillside. Windshield wipers were sweeping away what was only a minor inconvenience of moisture to the drivers. To me, the same moisture could represent the difference between a cozy night spent in the woods, and one most miserable.

When the traffic cleared I walked across Route 30.

In the early pioneer days of America, travel from place to place was done mostly over trails. These trails were often given colorful names by the people who blazed or improved them. As the trails grew in size to become roads, they still were known by their popular names.

This system of personalized roads worked well while the automobile was still in its youth. But, as traffic increased, and roads began to overlap, a better system of identification was needed. In 1925, the federal government implemented a highway numbering system. Today, with the names of roads slowly slipping from memory, modern highway systems are largely known by their assigned numbers.

Before it was identified as Route 30, this famous road was widely known as The Lincoln Memorial Highway.

In 1912, Carl Fisher had a dream for this country: to build a graveled road that spanned the country from the Atlantic Ocean to the Pacific. It was an ambitious idea. Roads at that time were decent around towns and cities. But in the great stretches that divided civilized places, most highways were deplorable. They were dusty in clear weather, and muddy when wet. If weather conditions worsened, many were impassible.

To many, the idea of a graveled, tended road, which reached across the country, was nonsense; but to Carl

Fisher the idea was workable. He reasoned that for the benefit of being situated along the nation's first coast-to-coast highway, communities of the proposed route would provide the necessary equipment to build it.

Rather than completely build a new road, Fisher worked out a plan to connect existing roads, where possible, in order to make the most direct route. In many instances the highway went right through the center of a town. As a result, small villages would become bustling towns. Hotels, inns, garages and stores would soon spring up all along the highway.

Public excitement began to build. Fisher called his idea the Coast-to-Coast Rock Highway. But Henry Joy, president of the Packard Motor Car Company, came up with an idea of naming the highway in memory of Abraham Lincoln. At the time, Congress was considering spending $1.7 million on a marble memorial. Joy urged Fisher to write Congress and suggest that a coast-to-coast highway would be a better memorial to the former President.

Fisher liked the idea. The renaming of the highway would inspire patriotism and increase revenue. The Lincoln Memorial Highway was born.

On October 31, 1913, folks from New York to San Francisco joined in a grand celebration as the transcontinental highway was dedicated. Some thought the highway would be unfurled in a few months time. Instead, the highway was connected piece-by-piece, state-by-state for more than a decade. Dusty roads were covered by concrete as a ribbon across the country began to take shape.

The road was finally completed in 1927. On Saturday, September 1, 1928, thousands of Boy Scouts, from New York to San Francisco, installed small concrete markers, about one every mile. These markers bore the bust of the sixteenth President and the inscription, "This Highway Dedicated to Abraham Lincoln."

Today, travelers who are driving east and west across the country take faster, four-lane highways. These modern roads do not drive through towns; they pass around them. The bustle that the Lincoln Memorial Highway brought to many small towns was passed to exit-ramp communities. But the road has not died off. There are many organizations existing today that work to keep the memory of this famous highway alive.

I crossed the Lincoln Memorial Highway in a faint drizzle. Traffic was heavy and so I did not have an opportunity to linger long on this historical road. The hard paved surface felt foreign to my feet, which hurried me across it.

Reentering the woods I was greeted with a shuddering peal of thunder. Judging from the darkening hue of the sky, and the sounds beginning to erupt from the heavens, I knew that I did not have much time before the rain would begin again. With less than a mile to the shelter area, I began to walk as fast as I could without breaking into a run.

At the top of a small ascent, I reached the wooden sign indicating that the shelter area was just off the trail. Turning east, I quickly made my way back the blue blazed trail. The first shelter that I reached was the same one that I had reserved. I eased my backpack to the shelter floor and saw that the previous visitors had left behind a small stack of firewood. I was grateful for their gift, but needed to collect more for the night.

Taking no time to rest I made haste to the firewood pile. The clouds seemed so filled with rain that I feared any sudden movement or noise on my part would unleash the coming storm. Filling my arms with firewood, I trudged to the shelter, dropped the load, and repeated the process several more times. My legs and feet were aching terribly and I was out of breath from carrying the firewood. Yet, knowing the rainstorm was only minutes away, I did not want to stop until the task was completed.

Finally, when it appeared I had enough wood to get me through the night, I entered the shelter and eased myself to the hard wood floor. No sooner had I taken my first, unlabored breath than the rain tore through the weakened skies and poured down upon the forest. I pushed my backpack against the shelter wall and leaned my back into it as if it were a pillow. Swinging both legs to the floor before me I let out a long sigh that sounded more of a cry of anguish than of relief.

The rain pounded through the trees and began to transform unseen depressions into small pools. Little trails become tiny streams that found each other in the maddening rain. Soon miniature rivers were formed all around the camp.

I watched the water roll and push around me. The sensation of being warm and dry inside of the shelter was indescribable. Had my arrival been postponed for even a few minutes I would have been caught in the downpour. My clothing would have become soaked again and I would be faced with the added task of drying everything out for the night.

Even though the lean-tos are open-aired and crudely fashioned, they provide the very thing most needed on days like this: shelter from the elements. Whether it is a log wall, snow igloo, or a stretched nylon sheet, any barrier raised between man and the out-of-doors on a stormy night is a relief.

After a brief rest, I pulled from my backpack my fire-blackened coffeepot, and set it outside of the boundaries of the shelter. Within minutes it was filled with rainwater. I filtered the contents and replenished the supply in the same manner. I was glad for the free gift of rainwater that saved me from the job of retrieving it from the hand pump.

From the small pile of firewood that had been found in the shelter, I found enough kindling to create a fire. With just a little coaxing I soon had a warm blaze glowing in the stone fireplace of the shelter. I changed into some dry clothing and strung my damp garments near the fire to dry. My boots were thoroughly wet but I could not set them out to dry until it was time to turn in.

Within a half hour of its beginning, the rainfall ceased and the sun, though low in the sky, began to shed its light once more across the forest. I ventured from the shelter to stretch and explore. Checking the shelters I found that I was alone at the site.

I decided to walk to the privy for an inspection of the facilities, and to walk out the tired kinks in my stiffening body. Stepping over the water puddles I began making the slight descent down the path toward the privy area. Though I had covered about fourteen miles without incident this day, the powers that direct the happenstance of man were about to break their prolonged silence.

Stepping down the incline, I placed my right boot on a jutting rock. Before I realized what was happening the rock broke free from the mud and slid downward. As if in slow motion, I fell backward and to my right side. Though I had plenty of time to realize that I was falling, there was not enough to do anything productive about it.

As falls go this one was not too bad. My body twisted to the right, and then I very gently – almost casually – slid down the muddy grass. I came to a soft rest after just a few feet of sliding. Before arising, I congratulated myself on handling the incident with such remarkable grace, and marveled that it had gone so smoothly.

Immediately, I stood up and shook myself to assure that I was not injured. Feeling no pain, I instinctively began to brush my pants when I felt the familiar texture of Pennsylvania mud. Twisting around, I looked down at my backside and saw a muddy streak reaching from my right pant leg to my hip.

I am not a swearing man. Had I been, then I might have searched the lower echelon of forbidden words to find one suitable for expressing my disagreement. But calling down a curse would have been useless. Besides, I was grateful for not having twisted an ankle.

I decided to finish my trip down the incline and wash my hands at the hand pump. As I continued my descent, I heard a loud bang. I immediately recognized the sound as that of the privy door swinging closed. Apparently I was not alone.

Walking toward the hand pump, I spied a woman leaving the privy station. She saw me at about the same time and flashed a friendly smile. I returned the greeting in likewise fashion and continued walking to the hand pump. She seemed to redirect her steps my way, stopping just a few feet from me.

She was a slender, handsome woman, maybe a few years my junior. She was very neatly attired in a sleeveless cotton shirt, denim shorts, and very smart, brown leather hiking boots. Her sandy blond hair was pulled into a ponytail that extended through the back of her blue Mickey Mouse ball cap. A small fanny pack and water bottle was strapped to her waist. Her healthy tan told me she was not a stranger to the out-of-doors, yet she did not exude a rugged appearance.

"How are you doing today?" I asked as I began to work the lever of the pump.

"Just fine, thank you" she replied, flashing another

friendly smile. "And you?"

There was something unique in the way she spoke. It was deliberate, and without colloquialism, as if she were paying careful attention to each syllable. This gave her an aura of refinement and intelligence. Her speech intrigued me.

"Doing well," I said over the squeaking of the hand pump. "Are you out for a day-hike?"

"Yes, I started this afternoon at Route 30. I went that way for a couple of hours," she said waving in a northerly direction, "and now I'm walking back to my car."

I stopped talking while I continued priming the pump with the lever. I thought she would walk away but she seemed to be in no hurry.

"It's a great day to be out walking, isn't it?" I asked.

"Oh, it is," she responded. "I like to come out here to walk and think. It helps me clear my mind."

"That it does," I replied.

Her remark made me wonder if this could be the woman who the father and son that I spoke with on my first day told me about.

"Were you by any chance walking a couple of days ago?" I asked. "I ran into a fellow and his son and they said that they were talking with a lady who was out day-hiking to 'clear her mind'."

The young woman's smile broke into an easy laugh. "That would be me! I recall talking with a man and his boy. If I remember correctly, they were heading to Ohiopyle. We stopped and talked for a while. He scolded me for walking alone."

"Well, it doesn't look like the scolding did much to discourage you," I laughed.

"Not in the least," she quickly replied.

"So were you able to clear your mind?" I asked.

For a nanosecond her bright eyes dimmed. I had asked the question in jest, but it had obviously become something much more invasive. It had rejuvenated something – some question – some thought – some trouble – that was stored inside of her, and which had been temporarily laid to rest by our conversation. Now, I had awakened it. I instantly regretted my impetuous question but could not recall it.

How much more walking would she have to do to put it back in its place? How much longer would she have to linger among the patient trees, until she had championed her thoughts?

Then suddenly, as quickly as it had dimmed, her face brightened again. And the twinge of guilt that I was beginning to feel was completely forgiven as the smile returned fully to her soft face. Clearly, she was unbeaten by this. Her appearance said so.

"I most certainly did!" she responded cheerfully.

Just then water started to pour from the spigot. I let go of the lever and began to wash my hands. It dawned on me that what intrigued me most about this young woman was indeed her appearance. Hiking alone in the woods would seem to demand of any woman a certain rugged bravery. Though I would not challenge her bravery, I found nothing rugged in the way she looked. On the contrary, she was quite feminine – dainty one might say.

"Did you get caught in any of the rain today?" I asked, changing the unspoken subject.

"It rained a little after I began, but not for very long. Then, as I was passing the shelter area on my way back, it started again. That's when I decided to duck in there and wait it out!" She punctuated her last sentence with another smile and pointed in the direction of the privy.

"Do you have any rain gear?" I asked as the flow of water ceased. I grasped the lever and began to work the pump again.

"Yes, I carry a plastic poncho, but I didn't have to use it today." She replied while watching my activity with evident interest.

As I finished washing my hands I looked up and smiled at my cute visitor. As she smiled in return, I saw her eyes catch the mud stain on my pants and follow it to my boot. The smile never left her face.

"Been out on the trail long?" she asked innocently.

Suddenly I became keenly aware of my appearance. It had been four days since I last showered and shaved. I had ascended steep hills until my entire body was saturated in sweat and then bedded down at night in those same clothes. Other than a few drops of waterless soap to disinfect my hands before eating, I had taken no steps to sanitize myself along the trail. And though I could not detect it, I could well imagine that a certain odor hung thickly about me.

"Well," I began, "I started four days ago in Ohiopyle. I'm heading to the northern end of the trail in Seward. I hope to be there in two more days."

"That's terrific!" she replied. "I'd love to try that myself sometime." Then she asked the question that I think she was straining to ask. Looking at my leg again she asked, "Did you take a tumble?"

I hoped my stubble-covered face concealed the warm flush. "Yeah, about two minutes ago I slipped on a rock while coming down here. I didn't hurt myself – just got a little muddy."

I had replied while twisting slightly backward to look at my dirty pants. In this movement the air pocket between us changed and I sensed the faint smell of perfume.

The perfume caught me off guard. It surprised me. It confused me. Suddenly, I was spirited out of the woods and deposited several places all at the same time. I was back in

Algebra class beside the pretty blond cheerleader. I was in my '72 Plymouth Duster fumbling with 8-track tapes, and singing loudly with the girl beside me. I was standing at my mailbox opening a greeting card and feeling a tickling sensation deep in my belly as I caught a whiff of perfume splashed on it many miles away.

Having lived alone since my divorce, I sometimes forget the benefits of feminine influence. I have forgotten how a darkened room can suddenly be lit by a graceful entrance. I have forgotten how a furrowed brow can be straightened by a simple touch. I have forgotten what perfume is, and what a nose can do.

"Well, I need to get back to camp and make some supper" I said while air-drying my hands. "You're welcome to join me if you wish."

"Oh, thank you. But I really must be going. I hope you have a good evening," she cheerfully replied with perfect accentuation, "and a wonderful trip!"

"Thanks. Enjoy your walk!" I turned from the hand pump and began walking towards the lean-to. As I ascended the small knoll I glanced in the direction of my exiting friend. She was making her way in the direction of the trail, moving through the thinly populated woods. Her steps seemed effortless. I saw no puddle being splashed, or twig being snapped. Softly she moved through the woods. An air of grace seemed to go with her.

When I reached the lean-to, I stirred the fire and threw some small logs on it. I changed into clean pants and checked my wet garments hanging near the fire. I then took time to organize my camp and put everything in order. After that I was more than ready to tend to the needs of my growling stomach.

I cooked supper, and, having been greatly nourished by the hot meal, finally settled back to relax. The late afternoon rain clouds had moved on, being replaced by a dimming orange sky. I sensed that it was a glorious sunset. But deep in the forest, beneath the rich canopy, I could only see slivers of colorful light playing far above me.

As daylight lost its predictable struggle, and nightfall crept noiselessly through the forest, I put away my cooking utensils and made final preparations for the quiet hours. In lieu of conversation, I occasionally provoked my burning companion with a short stick. It angrily answered with a shower of sparks and plume of smoke. Finally, I loaded the fire with heavy logs for the night and crawled into my sleeping bag.

Listening to the music of the crackling fire, I watched its light dance round the interior of the shelter while feeling strength slowly ebb from my body. Finally, as the power of night tipped the scales of my resistance, I fell soundly asleep.

Day Five

I could not figure out how the moose got into the lean-to. I discovered it in the back, down on all fours, simply staring at me with its large brown eyes. The sight of the large bovine creature in the shelter seemed so ridiculous that I began laughing out loud. The noise of my laughter startled the antlered animal. Jumping up it began to kick around, its hooves slipping on the slick wooden floor looking for a way to get out. That seemed even more hilarious to me, and I laughed all the harder.

The sound of my own laughter woke me. For a brief moment I opened my eyes and raised my head. The sunlight was already pouring into the lean-to. I lay my head back down on the pillow, closed my eyes, and started laughing some more.

Laughing myself awake is a trait that I have clearly inherited from my mother. Many times the sound of her own laughter over a crazy dream would shake her from her sleep. She would then wake my father, who, with greater patience than enthusiasm, would listen to her describe the dream that led to her hysterics. I do not believe that he ever found the same level of humor in the situation – but he was generally a good sport about it.

The night had passed by uneventfully. Twice I had

ventured from my sleeping bag to feed the fire, but immediately fell asleep upon returning to my hard bed. Whatever night sounds may have erupted, or however the nocturnal creatures may have stirred, they simply could not compare to my profound slumber.

A choir of birds in the trees above welcomed me as I finally emerged from my sleeping bag. The sun was shining brightly and the air seemed to be warming quickly. It was an unimpaired summer morning.

The fire had dimmed too low to rejuvenate easily. So, I cooked my breakfast on my backpacking stove. My clothing, which had become wet in yesterday's rain, had dried overnight by the fire. But the linings of my boots were still damp. It was terribly uninviting to feel the wet boot tightening around my stocking feet as I secured the lacings.

While packing away my things I began to notice how dirty everything was becoming. Nothing was immune to the grime any longer. My boots and clothing had dragged mud into the lean-to. My movements scattered it about until it attached itself to everything else. My clothing was soiled and my gear was filthy. I was sleeping in a dirty bag upon a dirty pad. Even my plastic eating utensils that I had kept in a closed plastic bag seemed to be mucky.

My hands were dirty, my face was soiled, and I could sense that my hair was beginning to take on amusing shapes whenever I pulled my cap off. I was glad not to have had a mirror. The last I saw of my reflection was when I closed my van door and caught a glimpse of myself in the window. That was five days ago. I was not that clean anymore; and in some ways I was not even that same man anymore.

I regretted not bringing a chamois camp towel. I could have used it to give myself a bath of sorts. Even a cold-water wash at the hand pump would have done wonders to make me feel better. The thought of an impending hot shower – in just over twenty-four hours – was really beginning to feel enticing. Soap, water, and shampoo never really seem like coveted objects – until one goes without them. And as I busied myself with breaking camp, my mind wandered often to the rejuvenating effects of my next shave.

Today would be the longest hiking day of the trip. I hoped to cover the nearly twenty miles to reach the Decker Ave Shelters – more commonly known as the Route 56 Shelter Area. I felt up to the task, and, with my backpack now lighter, I remained wonderfully optimistic about the day.

After filling my water containers I followed the short, side-trail from the Route 30 Shelters, and turned north on the Laurel Highlands Hiking Trail. The coolness of the morning was quickly dissipating beneath the warming sun. Though I could not fully see the sky it looked like it was going to be a grand summer day.

I did not complete ten steps when I walked into – literally – my first obstacle of the day: a spider's web. Spanning the breadth of the trail, like a fishnet that had been cast into the sea was a small web, dredging the currents of air for an unsuspecting victim. These nearly invisible strands mark the difference between living and dying for the smallest of God's creatures, and are encountered often along the trail.

I walked a few more steps and engaged another web that was stretched across my path. I sidestepped it, but as I continued walking, found myself passing through, or around, quite a few of them. Until today I had encountered only a small number of spider's webs along the trail. Now it was replete with them. There were simple cobwebs strung across the trail, and finely woven orb webs poised like a catcher's mitt between blades of grass. Some of them still carried moisture from the early morning's dew, while others had been sheltered, and were more difficult to see. It was of the latter category that I walked into that made me pause: a huge orb web suspended along the left side of the trail by long threads of invisible silk running at just below face level.

Webs are so commonplace that we rarely pause to enjoy the grand wonder that they display. That is indeed a shame for they are quite splendid.

The orb web begins as a spider ascends a fixed structure, such as a small vertical tree or plant. When the wind blows it releases a length of thread. If the spider senses that the length of thread has caught something – like another tree – it cinches up the silk, and fixes the starting point. This creates a bridge of sorts, which allows the spider to cross, while releasing a looser strand of silk. The looser strand is next fixed to a bottom point. The spider then begins to anchor the web at various points creating the frame of the web. Radius threads are laid out from the center to the frame, which are then strengthened by spiral threads of silk. Finally, the *coup de grâce*: inwardly-laid, sticky threads of silk, designed to ensnare the spider's prey.

Spider's silk is made up of amino acids, making it a thread of protein. It is surprisingly strong. By weight it is five times stronger than steel, and twice as durable as the Kevlar used in bullet-proof vests. It can stretch thirty per cent longer than its original length without tearing. Countless hours of research and study have been dedicated to the spider's silk in an effort to reproduce it in a marketable form. Though some significant strides have been made in creating synthetic silks, none can produce it more efficiently and quickly than the tiny, eight-legged

Araneae.

In my estimation, I do not possess any unusual phobia of the tiny creatures. But the thought of these quick-moving legs crawling around my body is wholly uninviting. So, I brushed the web from my face, left shoulder, and chest, and did a quick scan for the presence of the spider. Not finding it, I tried to continue my journey. But, after a few steps I caught, from the corner of my eye, sudden movement on my left forearm. Indeed, the spider was present, and was moving upward at an alarming pace. It was brown, and, for the moment, seemed exceedingly large. It withstood my first few attempts at shaking it off, and continued its rapid ascent up my arm.

I removed my ball cap and used it to begin beating wildly about my left arm and shoulder. At the same time I started to back up and twist myself in a circle, as if engaged in a life and death struggle with one of the forest's more formidable denizens.

Gone from my mind were the contemplative thoughts of the splendid spider and its ability to spin a magnificent, mysterious web. Instead, I became fixed upon the sole purpose of defending myself against the terrifying advances of the silent, creeping carnivore, which, I was now convinced, was entirely entrenched upon the goal of reaching the delicate portions of my neck and head.

With one of my swings, I dislodged the multi-legged beast from my arm only to see it bounce to my lower abdomen. For a moment, we both stood motionless, looking into the others unblinking eyes. I was not encouraged by its impression of intent. As it resumed its ascent across my body I was persuaded that the devil himself was set upon me, and I reacted with due force.

With an ungoverned fever, I resumed to beating myself with my cap while thrashing to and fro across the trail in an effort to dislodge myself from its death grip. From my throat, I heard ineloquent yelps and groans of primeval origin pouring forth. No longer able to take flight, I stood now to fight.

When it seemed that I might be losing my battle, I finally landed a swat on my chest that sent the untamed predator sailing through the air from me. Relieved of the threat, I returned my cap to my head like a sword to its sheath, and did a nervous little jig that resembled the body's reaction to a chilling wind. It was not until I began whirling my arms in the air, removing the invisible threads of web stretching across my body that I became struck with the sense of no longer being alone.

Glancing rearward, I saw the figure of a man standing just a few paces behind me on the trail. He was about my age, wearing spandex shorts, a nylon T-shirt, and trail running shoes. He carried on his back a hydration pack, and across his face, a perplexed look. Judging from that look, I sensed that he had must have been a spectator to my harrowing ordeal.

"Spiders." I said.

I heard in my own voice an inflection that echoed a sober warning – as if I had just discovered the fresh tracks of a grizzly bear.

"Oh," he responded. There was a certain caution in his voice. Yet I did not think it was directed toward any threat that he felt about the presence of spiders.

For the next few moments he just stood on the trail looking as if he were trying to make an important decision.

To break the awkward silence I asked, "Out for a run?"

"Yeah," he answered.

"Looks like you're going to have a nice day for it," I continued, trying to make my voice sound casual.

"Yeah, I think so," he agreed without looking up at the sky.

"How far are you going?" I inquired.

"Well, my wife dropped me off at Route 30 this morning, and is going to pick me up at Route 271 later today," he responded.

"Wow, that's a pretty good jog!" I said.

My new friend smiled and took a step in my direction. It seemed that my coherent speech was beginning to relieve him of the concerns that my former antics might have created.

"Thanks," he continued, "about ten miles I figure. This is the first time I've ever been on this trail. My wife grew up in this area, and for years has been telling me about it. We came up for a few days to visit her home, and before heading back, I thought I'd come out for a day of running."

"You're not from around here?" I asked.

"I'm from New York, but we live in Atlanta now." He replied. "How about you - where are you from?"

"I grew up just a few miles from here, and still live nearby. I've hiked the trail in sections before, but have never done a thru-hike. 'Been hiking for a few days now and am looking to finishing it tomorrow." I answered.

"Sounds cool!" he remarked. Then with a look of concern on his face he asked, "You doing alright?"

"Oh yeah," I assured him. "I walked into a spider's web and the thing was crawling all over me."

"Yeah, you gotta' watch those things," he said with a smile. "Well, I guess I really need to keep going." he said as he began to move past. "I hope your walk goes well!"

"Thanks!" I replied. "Have a good run!"

I stepped aside and let him pass me on the trail. He then began to jog northward. Whether or not he had any trouble with spider webs, I will never know. But after he passed in front of me, I did not encounter anymore.

I watched my visitor jog off at a steady pace. Trail running is becoming increasingly popular for those who like a good challenge, and have grown tired of the treadmills or city streets. The Laurel Highlands Hiking Trail is commonly used by runners, and provides a unique racetrack each summer for a very grueling race: the Laurel Highlands Ultra.

On the second Saturday of each June runners set out to run the entire length of the trail. Some do it alone, while others approach it in teams. The popularity of the race has grown over the years, attracting more than just local runners.

The Butchko brothers – Joe and Paul – had discovered the trail in the late 70s, and found it a nice place to run. In 1979 they gathered a few of their friends and tried running all seventy miles in one day. None of them made it past the 57th mile – which is an incredible feat in my estimation. The following year they returned for another race with seven other contestants. Four of the nine who started the race completed it – and that became the first official race, which has been ongoing since then.

I can scarcely imagine trying to run the trail in one day. Yet, not only do many runners complete the trail, some have even finished it in less than eleven hours. The very thought of that makes my feet hurt – as if they would need anything else to assault them on this fine summer day. So, I pushed the thought of running out of my mind and continued walking.

Though I could not see them, I began following the northern steps of my running visitor. My pace was not nearly as quick as his, but I was no less determined to enjoy the sense of being out-of-doors, and accomplishing a satisfying goal.

The sun was quickly melting away the night's moisture that was left clinging to the grass and small ferns at my feet. Though it was only mid-morning, the forest was beginning to heat up. I considered converting my hiking pants into shorts by un-zippering the pant legs. But the possibility of a tick leaping off of the high grass and unto my legs seemed too great. Instead, I sucked more frequently at my hydration pack, allowing the water to cool my system from the inside.

Within minutes of meeting the runner I reached one of the most history-filled landmarks along the Laurel Highlands Hiking Trail: Forbes Road. The trail intersects this important milestone at the foot of a wooden sign that plainly marks the juncture. As always, I paused at the intersection to enjoy the aura of the history-soaked road.

General John Forbes was born in Scotland in 1707. He became an officer in the Scottish Cavalry of the British army. When the French and Indian War broke out, Forbes was sent to North America to join the fight. In 1757 he received orders to lead an expedition to Fort Duquesne – present day Pittsburgh – and expel the French.

Two years earlier, General Edward Braddock had also made an attempt on Fort Duquesne. From Cumberland, Maryland his crew cut Braddock's Road to just seven miles short of their objective. On July 9, 1755, the French, and their Indian allies from Fort Duquesne, ambushed Braddock's troops. Braddock's forces were beaten back, and Braddock was mortally wounded. He died four days later. Fearing that his enemies might desecrate his grave, his remains were hurriedly buried in an unmarked grave beneath the road that he had built.

Forbes would also give his life to the same project. Yet, unlike Braddock, he would emerge victorious. History would suggest that he was not a better leader, more charismatic, or more intelligent than Braddock. They were both well-trained and highly educated British officers who followed the same European rules of warfare. It seems that the only advantage that Forbes had over Braddock was the lessons he was able to learn from Braddock's mistakes.

Forbes decided against following the same road to the French. Instead he followed Col. Burd's road to just west of present-day Bedford, Pennsylvania. From there he began to forge a new crossing directly over the mountains. Unlike Braddock, Forbes constructed fortifications and encampments along the way to provide protection, and to continue his supply lines. He was also careful not to engage his enemy prematurely. His work, however, would still not be easy.

Laurel Mountain was a solid obstacle, and not one easily surmounted by Forbes. Much planning went into deciding a route over the ridge. As work began, it seemed that nature itself would not comply. One of the rainiest seasons in anyone's memory came upon the workers in 1758, drenching them without mercy. The roadbed became flooded. Supply wagons were marooned, and sickness befell the workers. Even Forbes himself became so ill that he directed the work and led his men from a litter being carried between two horses.

By November of 1758, Forbes phenomenal efforts had brought him to Fort Ligonier, just 40 miles southeast of the French. Although a decision had been made to wait out the winter in Fort Ligonier, news reached Forbes that their fortune had suddenly changed. The French who had been entrenched at Fort Duquesne were in dire straits. Their supply lines from the north had been cut off by other British advances and a great number of their Indian allies had deserted for the winter.

Immediately upon hearing the condition of his enemies, Forbes launched an attack. As his forces neared Fort Duquesne, the French found that they could not withstand. They deserted their posts and set the fort afire. Still gravely

ill, Forbes took possession of the prized fort and renamed it
Fort Pitt, in honor of British Prime Minister William Pitt.

Forbes health began declining rapidly. He remained in
Fort Pitt another month and then began the arduous journey
to Philadelphia. His efforts firmly established him in the
American history books, but the effort cost him his life: he
died just three months later.

Forbes Road remained an essential artery for many
years. Rugged as it was, it still provided a more direct and
safer way to reach the Ohio River – which had long been
recognized as the gateway to the west. Eventually,
smoother and more direct paths won the allegiance of
travelers, and the forest began to reclaim the rugged scar
cut across the mountain. Yet, in places like this, it can still
be observed and relished.

As I reached Forbes Road – now just a thinly cut path
through the woods – I lowered my pack to the ground to
rest for a moment. Gazing up and down the road I tried
imagining the sights and sounds that would have greeted
me in Forbes' day. I pictured the bright red uniforms of the
British troops marching smartly past me, and the
primitively-clad southern Cherokee and Catawba Indian
braves who had joined Forbes' forces. I strained to hear
echoes of the merry fife that must have resounded in these
woods, and the repetitious drum beat that provided even
tempo to the soldiers' boots. These ghost sights and sounds
marched past me in parade-like order while I saluted with a
slight nod of my head.

As the imagined sounds passed me, I knelt down and
dug my hand into the soil. I felt the dirt where Generals
Forbes, Washington, and Bouquet may have stood to confer
over what must have seemed to them an uncertain future.
Now, we read their exploits knowing their outcomes. But
they stood in those uncertain times without the advantage

of our hindsight, and made choices that not only secured their places in history, but our futures as well.

Laurel Mountain is just one of many crucibles wherein the forging of this nation took place. This stretch of woods appears unremarkable by any method of interpretation, yet its contribution to history has made it a sanctified crossing to those who pause to reflect and recount.

After a brief rest I returned my pack to my back and crossed Forbes Road. Instantly I was swallowed by the twists and turns that mark the Laurel Highlands Hiking Trail.

Having eaten most of my groceries since the outset of my hike, my backpack was theoretically lighter. But as I began to encounter the first of the many small hills, I lost touch with that reality. It was becoming a torturously hot day – easily the hottest of the week. Sweat was soon pouring from my body, soaking my clothing. I was trying to keep myself adequately hydrated. So, as I struggled against gravity's unyielding demands on the hillsides, I began drawing at my water supply.

Occasionally I passed small blueberry bushes holding out their ripened fruit. Whenever I found them I paused to forage. Their sweet, wet taste was quite refreshing. As I ate some of the forest's produce, I remembered the days when my mother would send me and my brothers out into the woods to gather wild strawberries or blackberries. We were given specific instructions not to return home until our coffee cans were full. None of us relished the chore. So, ingenious as we were, we discovered that the easiest way to fill our cans was to steal berries from the cans of our siblings. Naturally, this resulted in many quarrels, none of which our mother could completely resolve, since none of us was more innocent than the other.

Near the middle of the morning, I encountered two men

and a woman resting along the trail. They appeared to be in their early twenties, and were dressed in jeans and T-shirts. They were equipped with notebooks and pencils and had been pouring over them as I approached. They told me that they were there on behalf of the State, and were conducting a wildlife habitat evaluation. Since they seemed rather busy, I did not linger to talk, but continued my northward trek.

Other than the occasional squirrel or chipmunk, I had not witnessed much in terms of wildlife. However, animal tracks were abundant in the dried mud along the trail. These were mostly left by deer, raccoon, skunk or possum. Canine prints were also found. Though they might have been left by coyotes, many dogs are brought by their owners to hike the trail.

As I stepped out into a natural clearing a crow burst from the lower branches of a maple tree. Two blackbirds were above, taking turns swooping down upon it. The crow had likely raided the nest of the blackbirds, or had invaded a feed. Though it was easily twice their size, it was no match for their quick darting movements, and could only try to make an effective retreat.

Slowly the crow gained altitude and speed, but the blackbirds kept up their attack. With each pass of the crow they appeared to be able to inflict another peck with their sharp beaks. The crow cawed out in protest, but until it could gain some altitude, and then swap that for speed in a quick dive, it had no meaningful defense. I listened to the complaint of the crow and audibly followed the attack through the woods until I saw the blackbirds silently returning to the clearing. It was simply another day in the life of a living forest.

Throughout the morning I pressed on, ascending each hill until nearly breathless while feeling the backs of my thighs and buttocks screaming in protest. As I rounded these many small hills and began the descent on the other side, my quadriceps would absorb the punishment and register their objection. This cycle was repeated many times over as the sun teased me with its unending heat, effectively draining me of my physical resources.

Eventually, to my great relief, I noticed a gradual darkening of the sky. The weather on Laurel Hill can be fluid. At times there is no noticeable seam between rain or sun or snow. Without notice or warning, conditions can change rapidly. It was beginning to appear that I would be getting some relief from the heat in the form of a shower.

As the first few drops hit me, I stopped and put a cover over my pack. Being drenched in my own sweat, I was looking forward to the warm summer shower and its cooling effect.

Within minutes the soft patter of rain began sounding out on the leafy canopy above me. The tempo of the sound quickly increased and I began to feel the water on my bare arms and face. It was indeed a welcomed sensation. Although the sky was threatening with a viciously dark color, the rain increased only to a light and steady shower.

As I walked through the delightful shower, and turned a bend on the trail, I was met with a peculiar sight. Just off the trail, in a small grove of trees, a man was sitting on a fallen log. Above him was stretched a green plastic tarp held in place by small bungee cords that were attached to the surrounding branches. In the center of the tarp, he had raised a trekking pole, extended to its maximum length against the roof of the tarp.

The man was attired in gray hiking shorts and a light-tan T-shirt. His leather boots were worn, telling the tale of many dusty miles. On top of his head he wore a floppy safari hat that shielded a rotund, cheery face. That merry countenance was nearly encircled in a snow-white beard.

I waved to him as I approached. Flashing a broad, high-spirited smile, he waved in return, and motioned for me to step off of the trail.

"Come on out of the rain!" he called. The entire scene had piqued my curiosity, and so I accepted his invitation. Stepping off of the trail and ducking beneath his smart little canopy, I returned his smile.

"Where ya heading?" he inquired in an animated voice.

"Going end-to-end," I replied. "I expect to finish up at Seward tomorrow - how about you?"

"End-to-end myself - started two days ago in Seward, and am headin' south for O-Hi-O-Pyle." He stretched out the last word in a singsong sort of way. "Got rained on yesterday and decided that I didn't want any of that today. So, I built me a little shelter to wait it out!"

"Nice, real nice," I replied with genuine honesty as I glanced about his little oasis.

"Well, don't just stand there," he said laughingly, "have a seat!"

He had gestured towards another log that was beneath his make-shift umbrella. I unbuckled my backpack, slid it to the ground, and lowered myself onto the log that had been worn smooth by many summer suns. I let out a sigh. It had been nearly four hours since I had sat, and the change of posture brought waves of relief over my body.

"Well, now that's more like it!" he exclaimed with a great deal of satisfaction in his voice, "I'm about to have lunch – care to join me?"

"That sounds like a real good idea," I returned. "I haven't eaten all morning and am feeling pretty hungry."

I reached into my backpack and withdrew my food sack. I dug through its few remaining contents until I found a pack of cheese crackers. Having spent the last few days being jostled about in my sack, they had been reduced to an assembly of colored crumbs. I tore open the cellophane and poured a load of the small fragments into my hand.

"Don't tell me that's your lunch!" my new friend exclaimed. "You can't live out here on crumbs! Here, let me see what I have."

From his floppy backpack my bearded friend produced a very large bag. He untied a string at the top and let down the sides. The bag was a large, flat nylon tarp that had been tied up like a hobo's sack. As he opened the sack an incredible assortment of groceries spilled forth. I was amazed as to the quantity of food that he had. There were apples, oranges, dried fruit snacks, cheese blocks, beef sticks, noodles, rice, and beans. He had packs of dehydrated meals, oatmeal, powdered drink mixes, bags of candy bars, hardtack, and chocolate. There was a bag of bagels, a jar of peanut butter and small squeeze bottle of grape jelly. Other, smaller plastic bags were twisted shut, but were bulging with their hidden contents.

"You've got enough there to feed an army!" I said amazed. "Your pack must weigh over 60 pounds with all of that stuff!"

"Well, I don't come out here to starve myself to death!" He retorted with a laugh. From out of the mass of food he seized upon a small brick of pre-wrapped cheese and a meaty tube of treated beef. These he gave to me and then dove his hand back into the pile of food. From it he produced another brick of cheese and pepperoni tube for himself.

"Do you have a knife?" he asked.

"Yes, I do," I replied, "But I really don't want to take your food. I have my own to eat"

"Nah, don't worry about that" he returned. "It's not easy lugging all of this stuff around. You'll just make my load lighter if you eat some."

I had a sense that continued refusal would only serve to insult my merry host. So, I accepted his gift, and found my knife in my rucksack. I lopped off a slab of meat and put it between two generous sides of cheese. As I started to eat I was amazed how hungry I had become, and how good the provided meal was.

"How many days have you been out here?" My host asked with mouthfuls of pepperoni and cheese.

"I started late in the afternoon five days ago," I replied. "I guess if I pushed myself I could reach the end of the trail late today, but I'm not out to set any records. So, I'll finish it early tomorrow morning."

"Have you met many people out this past week?" He inquired as he carved out another large piece of meat.

"Well, a few," I answered. "But really not as many as I thought I'd meet. Sometimes in the summer the traffic gets really heavy, but I think I hit a slow week."

"Yeah, I met a fellow out running this morning, but no one else until you," he said. "And I didn't have any company at the shelters last night or the night before."

"You're by yourself, then?" I asked.

"Yep, I always go by myself. I prefer it that way. I don't hike fast and would only slow other people down."

"You've hiked this trail before?" I asked.

"Nope. First time. I heard about it from another feller' while hiking on the Appalachian Trail in Maryland. I made a note to walk it some day and so here I am!" He said with a good-natured laugh.

I sliced off another piece of beef stick and took a healthy bite at it. "Have you hiked the entire AT?"

"Tried to, but my knees gave out in northern Virginia. Later, I went back and hiked through Maryland and Pennsylvania, but never did finish the whole thing. Maybe some day."

"What was your trail name? Maybe I saw it on one of the trail logs." I asked.

He swallowed some cheese and then rinsed it down with some water from a plastic canteen. "They called me Santy Clause 'cause of my beard," he said laughingly.

I scanned my fading memory for a moment, "I can't recall reading your name on the register logs, or hearing about you. But I haven't been on that trail for a few years now. I'd like to go back someday and hike it some more. I've always enjoyed myself there."

Santy Clause nodded in agreement. He cut off some more cheese and then leaned back against a tree as if in contemplation. He then started telling me stories of the people he had met, and the good times he had shared with them. He told me stories of cold nights in Georgia, and steamy-hot days in Tennessee. He recounted bear sightings, rattle snake encounters, and terrifying thunderstorms. He laughed at all of his own stories and the smile never left his face – which he continually stuffed with food.

I had nearly finished the tube of beef stick when I realized that it had stopped raining. The sun was burning hot again, kicking up a steam in the forest.

"You know I hate to end this, but I probably ought to get going," I said.

"Well, don't run off until we have some dessert," he said as he untied one of his smaller plastic bags. From it he withdrew two thick chocolate brownies still wrapped in their store-bought plastic, and handed one to me.

"Are you sure I'm not taking your food for the week?" I asked with a measure of guilt that was weakening in the face of the deep chocolate.

"Nah! I always carry more than enough with me. I guess that's why I walk so slowly!" He said with a laugh.

I opened the chocolate dessert and took a bite. I had not tasted this kind of delicacy for days now, and so I savored it with slow deliberate movements of my mouth and tongue.

In two bites he devoured his brownie and washed it down with some more water. Santy Clause then looked at the brightening forest. "Well, if you're headin' off, I think I'll have myself a little snooze." He leaned his heavy frame against a tree behind the log that he was sitting upon.

"Well, I must thank for you for the great lunch!" I said as I stood up and harnessed myself into my pack. "It sure hit the spot!"

"Think nothing of it," he said with a reinforcing wave. "It's great that you wandered by at lunch time – I hate eating alone."

"I hope that the rest of your trip goes well!" I called as I stepped out from beneath his plastic rooftop.

"Same to you my friend!" he said with the never-ending smile.

As I took a few steps away I glanced backward. Santy Clause had his eyes closed and may have already slipped into the nether regions of suspended consciousness. His white beard certainly lent a St Nicholas appearance. But I believe what ultimately underwrote his merry moniker was the generosity of his spirit.

Within minutes of returning to the trail, I began to regret eating such a hearty lunch. With my belly full, and the returning sun beginning to warm my face, I was overcome by a wave of sleepiness. I kept pushing northward hoping that the exercise would rejuvenate me. Instead, it made me more tired. After a few miles, I simply could not take it anymore. So, I found a shaded spot beneath an elderly oak, and eased my backpack down against it. I then lowered my body to the ground and pressed myself into my bag until I found a comfortable spot.

The recrudescing sun was warming the forest, and the softly blowing wind was striking me in an incredibly inviting manner. I leaned my head back, drew my cap down over my face, and closed my eyes. Soon, I became lost to the material world about me as I made a visit to the wraithlike cosmos. There, dreams are as plentiful as leaves on a forested floor. I toyed with them leaving one for the pleasurable sights and sounds of another until I explored them all with a simple innocence. Occasionally a current of awareness jolted my body and I had a limited sense of physical existence. But it was soon smothered by the gentle beckoning of the nether voices, and I drifted merrily away again.

Without a clock it was difficult to judge how long I had slept. Nor was it important to me when I came to an understanding of my surroundings. When I eventually arose from the soft spot beneath the watchful oak, I felt as refreshed as having an eight hour sleep. I brushed the loose soil from my pants – a completely pointless act – and continued my northward portage with a renewed vigor.

The trail soon led me out of the woods and into an open, field-like section of tall weeds. The grassy meadow was only a short break in the continuum of the forested plain. But as I stepped out into the open it provided an opportunity to experience the true heat of the day. The constant protection of my tall wooded friends had spared me the intensity of the sun's labor. Unaccustomed to the bright light, I squinted my eyes as I quickly crossed the small opening. With satisfying relief I stepped back into the darkened, cool woods, and continued prodding along. But soon, the heat began to penetrate the forest as the golden sunlight dripped past the upper canopy of leaves. As I pressed forward, the sweat gathered in droplets all over my body until they were released into tiny torrents down my face, arms, legs and back. I nursed water from my hydration valve, but as the afternoon wore on, I began to suck in air bubbles. This was a sure sign that my water supply was running very low, and that I needed to conserve what I had left for the remaining trip.

I soon walked into an area known as "Mystery Hill." I have yet to find the reason for this strange name. There are other locations in Pennsylvania that bear the same or a similar name. Typically, these areas are so called because there is reported to be a gravitational abnormality associated with the location. For instance, in neighboring Bedford County, on the outskirts of New Paris, Pennsylvania, there is an area known as "Gravity Hill."

Many years ago, I had heard of Gravity Hill and drove to it to investigate. From Bethel Hollow Road to Gravity Hill Road, I crossed over a small knoll. Driving to what appeared to be the bottom of that hill, I placed my vehicle in neutral. To my utter amazement, the vehicle began to roll backwards – up the hill. Since then I have visited Gravity Hill a number of times and have always experienced the same thing. I have also noted that I always feel a little dizzy when I leave. However, I suppose that that may not mean much when one considers that I will become violently ill on a merry-go-round. But it adds to the mystery for me.

Mystery Hill along the Laurel Highlands may not share Gravity Hill's claim to fame. But on this date it felt as though gravity was working a little harder than usual.

It was a spectacular summer day, but the heat was really draining me. The trail was not overly difficult, but it often sent me over small hills that made me flush with perspiration. Unlike the southern section of the trail, which is marked by frequent streams and springs, I had encountered no water source along this day's walk. So, I sipped very sparingly at my depleting water supply. Each swallow was savored in my mouth before sending it to my stomach to be distributed to the many demands of a quickly dehydrating body.

During the mid-afternoon hours, I came across the Route 271 Shelter sign. I paused for a minute or two, considering whether or not I should walk back to the shelter for water. But the shelter area is nearly one mile off of the trail. That would add an additional two miles to what was already the longest day of the trip. I finally decided to continue prodding along. I thought that I would certainly encounter a water source along the way from which I could filter a fresh supply. Unbeknown to me at the time, there is no spring or stream found along this section of the trail.

Within minutes, I came to the last of the hardtop roads that the northbound trail crosses: Route 271 – The Menoher Highway. General Charles T. Menoher was born in 1862 in a section of Johnstown known then as Grubbtown. He graduated from West Point in 1886 and became a career army officer. He commanded the Rainbow Division in France during WWI, and maintained an outstanding record as an officer. His resignation in 1918 created a vacancy that was filled by Brigadier General Douglas MacArthur.

Menoher Highway was proposed just before Christmas in 1919. It was to lead from his birthplace near Franklin St. in Johnstown, cross over Laurel Mountain to Waterford, and end at Ligonier. Although there were some reservations concerning the construction of the highway, its proponents were hesitant to voice them. To contest the building of the road would be like insulting the hometown hero. Having wide support then, legislation for the road was soon passed, and construction began. Taking years to complete, the Menoher Highway was finally opened, and is now traveled by very few who can recall anything about the late General.

I stood on the General's highway for a moment to contemplate. But the heat reflecting off of the macadam became too unbearable. So, I very soon crossed the old hero's road and returned to my journeying.

After about an hour's walk, the trail left the woods to follow an old dirt road. As I left the protection of the forest, I once again felt the burning heat of the day. I pulled the brim of my ball cap down to just above my eyes to protect myself from the sunlight, and kept my eyes fixed on the ground to protect them from the glare. Looking down, I was surprised to see my boots kicking up dust. For days they had walked only along soften soil or atop the lush moss that often blankets the trail. Like my parched throat, my boots seemed annoyed with the changes that today's walk was now bringing.

As I walked along the dirt road, I noticed a white Chevy truck backed just off of the tram road and parked facing the trail. Immediately I recognized it as some type of utility, or work truck. There are numerous underground gas wells in this vicinity of the ridge, and it is not altogether uncommon to see a worker reading or checking one of the gas wells.

As I neared the truck I saw that it was indeed a gas company vehicle. The driver was seated inside and appeared to be doing some paper work. The engine was idling, and the driver was likely enjoying the benefits of the air conditioner on this hot day. As I drew closer, I noted that the driver was a female. I could tell that she saw me well in advance, and as I approached the vehicle, I noticed that she had been glancing in my direction.

I wondered if she were watching me because of my shoddy appearance. I was covered in dirt, terribly unkempt, and obviously quite worn out from my trip. Surely I was a sight. Or, my egocentric mind pondered, perhaps she was staring at me because she had never seen such a rugged backpacker before. Maybe she was enthralled with the sight of a lone man walking through the woods, fighting the elements for survival, forcing himself to move forward where a weaker person might falter. That was it, of course! She simply could not divert her attention from the sight of this hardy mountain man treading somewhere between one adventure and another. Why, my appearance to her must have been captivating, if not inspirational! I nearly blushed to think of the romantic images that I must have excited for her.

I sensed my back straightening beneath my backpack, and found that my steps lost a bit of their former weariness as they skipped with renewed passion. If it was the sight of a rugged, debonair outdoorsman that she was being entertained with, then I felt it was my momentary calling to provide nothing less.

I strode along the dirt road glancing one way and then another. My eyes swept the forest edge as if my very life depended upon my constant vigilance. I could sense my audience's attention as I neared the truck. Finally, reaching the vehicle I casually glanced her way in a nonchalant manner. She gave me a friendly smile and I returned the greeting with a polite, yet somewhat distant nod that was designed to stir her blood.

As I walked past the vehicle I could almost hear the excited story she would be telling her family that night:

> *"I saw a rugged man step out of the dark woods today with a heavy backpack and stroll tirelessly past my vehicle. He swaggered with a captivating confidence, and then as suddenly as he appeared, he slipped into the recesses of the forest's mysterious hollows."*
>
> *"How long do you think he's been out*

there?" her children would sing wide-eyed. "Probably for days, yes?"

"Oh, judging from his appearance I'd say he's been battling the harshest of elements for weeks - if not months!" would come her convincing reply, punctuated with a far-away look in her eyes.

I smiled over the mind game I was playing. The crunch of the gravel beneath my boots and the feel of the hot sun on my head were no longer noticeable in light of the entertainment I was creating for myself.

It was a few minutes after passing the white truck, while still caught up in my daydreaming, it dawned upon me that I had not seen a trail blaze in some time. I paused and looked down the road in front of me. Not seeing any I turned around and looked for blazes apparent to someone traveling in the opposite direction but saw nothing. It was obvious that I had walked off of the trail somewhere.

Turning around, I began to retrace my steps. I paused occasionally to look for the familiar yellow blazes marking the path, but could not find any. Eventually, I returned near the truck. The woman was still seated in the cab of the vehicle. She had been following my return with apparent interest. I glanced briefly her way as I passed the truck. She smiled once again and I gave her another genteel nod.

Walking just a few more minutes, I came across a yellow blaze. I continued southbound another twenty yards and encountered another one. This confirmed that I was again on the trail. So, I turned around and began walking northward again. A faded yellow blaze painted on an old tree confirmed that I was correctly moving north, but as I neared the white truck they seemed to disappear.

The female driver seemed to be fixed upon my efforts.

She watched my approach, and as I neared the truck I glanced at her again. She gave me another smile, but I knew the nod she got in return was lacking some of its former suaveness. I scanned the area, not for hidden dangers as before, but for yellow blazes that would again orient me. As I continued walking it did not take me long to realize that there were no more blazes, and that I was off of the trail again.

It took a great deal of effort to turn myself around and retrace my steps - not because I was growing tired. But, it was because I knew that I was becoming a curious spectacle to the quiet lady in the white truck.

Within minutes I neared the gas truck again. I was convinced that I was somehow losing the trail very near the vehicle, yet I could not discern where. My audience watched with obvious curiosity as I approached. As I passed again in front of the truck I looked her way. She smiled once more. I nodded weakly but quickly diverted my eyes.

Walking a few minutes down the dirt road I came across the yellow blazes again. I was utterly confused. Clearly, the trail was following the dirt road. Yet, there were no obvious portals where it turned off. It just seemed to disappear.

I had no choice but to turn around once more, and walk north looking for the trail. Sometimes when there is a lack of trees, blazes will be painted on large rocks. I searched everywhere for a blaze but found nothing. Soon, I approached the white truck. I could tell that the woman behind the wheel was watching me, and I had a sense that she was smiling too. I did not possess the courage to look her way, but walked past trying to pretend that I was in total control of my situation. This thin pretense, however, was not achieving its desired end.

I continued farther along the road than I had walked before hoping to find a blaze. But just as before, they had vanished.

I paused to consider my options; but there were really none to consider. The only choice that I had was to walk back to the truck and kindly ask the driver if she had any idea where I was. This, I knew, was not going to be an easy undertaking, and I silently prayed that I might be set upon by a wild bear before reaching the truck. At least that dilemma possessed less threatening consequences.

Turning around I trudged back the dirt road. There was no skip to my steps and I felt my back sagging once more beneath the backpack. I knew that the driver of the truck saw me coming. I could feel her stare, and I could only guess what she was thinking. However, before I reached the vehicle she apparently completed her paperwork. I saw her strap her seat belt on and then pull out. She turned south on the dirt road and bounced away from me. I stopped to watch her go and then to let the dust settle. Even though I was still lost, I felt wildly relieved knowing that I did not have to explain to her my situation.

The wind from my conceited sails was long gone. I now imagined quite a different conversation between the woman and her family when she arrived home:

> *"I saw a man stumble from the woods today, bent beneath a relatively light-looking backpack. He seemed pitifully disoriented as I saw him wander hopelessly up and down the trail."*
>
> *"Do you think he's been long in the woods?" her children would ask with grave concern for my being.*
>
> *"Oh, I have no doubt that this was his first*

day in the out-of-doors. "

After the truck rolled out of sight I continued walking along the road. I paused at the spot where the woman had been parked and glanced around. There, just beyond the place where the truck had been, I saw a small sign pointing to the trail. It had been concealed from me by the truck. Blushingly, I hurried over to it, and gladly stepped into the woods.

I continued my northward hike feeling completely exhausted. I had walked over fourteen miles this day and there remained another five before me. I was getting no more water out of the hydration tube, and was beginning to feel sick in my stomach from the lack of water and the intense heat. My head was also beginning to pound with each footfall. These were some of the earliest signs of heat exhaustion, and I desperately wanted to cool down. I was regretting my decision to hike all the way to Decker Ave Shelters.

The heavens above must have heard the pleas of my aching stomach - for, I soon noticed a blackening sky. At that moment there was nothing that I longed for more than a cool rain shower. I did not have long to wait. Before I walked another half mile the preliminary sprinkles of a waiting storm began to fall. For the second time today the unpredictable weather atop Laurel Mountain was having a change of mind.

For the next few miles, I walked through the rainstorm relishing every drop of moisture that washed over me. My drenched shirt felt like a cold compress against a body wracked by a sun-induced fever, and my parched mouth took some relief from the saturated air that I breathed. Soon, however, my enjoyment of the rain ended when my boots began filling with water once again. With each step, I could feel water pumping between my toes and could see it squeezing out of the sides of the boot.

As the downpour continued the pathway became more treacherous. At places the trail resembled a rushing streambed. Climbing the hillsides meant leaving the path to avoid the rushing water. This often forced me to crawl through branches and brush that was growing thick along the trail. This retarded my progress and added many more steps to my already aching feet. I once again began to rehearse my regret in bypassing the Route 271 Shelters – where I would have been comfortable and dry for hours now.

Constantly forward I trudged. The luster that my feet enjoyed in the morning had turned drab. Additionally, my spirit was also draining of its resources. At each turn in the trail, I expected to see the shelter sign, and felt dejected when I did not. Finally, I had to stop along the trail and lean my back against a tree in the rain. I stood there resting for a few minutes in the rain, feeling too tired to move ahead. Then, I glanced ahead. There, just thirty yards beyond my resting spot the Decker Ave Shelter sign seemed to materialize before me. The candle of my soul that I thought was extinguished flickered with renewed energy.

Thankfully, I turned off of the trail and began to make my way back to the shelter. I had never stayed at this location before and was hoping that the shelters were just off of the trail. Whether it was my extreme anxiety to finally reach the shelter area that seemed to prolong my agony, or that it does in fact lie well off the trail is still uncertain to me. The only thing I can recall about that walk was that it seemed painfully immeasurable.

Decker Avenue Shelter Area lies deep in a natural cut. Although I was initially blind to it, it is a remarkably beautiful site. A spring-fed stream courses through the shelter area giving it a very pleasant aura. The hydra pressure from the stream is great enough to continually feed a spigot that the Park has installed. The spigot is the shelter's centerpiece. In addition to being enjoyable to watch, the spigot meant there would be no hand pumping the night's water supply. But I barely noticed these things as I slumped into camp.

I had reserved the first shelter. Without pomp I dropped my backpack to its wooden floor and carefully lowered my backside down onto its creaking timbers. A heartfelt groan that had been capped in place for nineteen miles escaped my lips like water from an artesian well. I unlaced my muddy boots and released their soggy prisoners. Lifting my pulsing feet to the hardwood floor I stretched out my legs and began apologizing profusely to them. They had carried me further than usual, and though they complained often and loudly, they did not let me down.

Leaning into my backpack I closed my eyes and rested while the slowing summer rain beat out a rhythm in the forest. I had plenty of time to make camp and explore my surroundings. My first order of business was to take an old-fashioned rest.

When I opened my eyes the rain had completely stopped and the soft sounds of a living forest could be heard over the gurgling stream. I stretched out my stiff legs and walked to the spigot where I drew fresh water. Drinking my fill, I returned to the shelter and set upon the task of gathering firewood. There was no wood left over by the previous occupants of the shelter and so I inspected some of the other lean-tos hoping to find some dry wood. I returned empty handed and was relinquished to gather wood from the wood pile. This, however, had been completely soaked by the rain, and I feared that I might have a hard time building my evening's fire.

When I had gathered enough firewood for the night, and found what seemed to be the driest of kindling, I returned to the shelter and made camp. Atop my camp stove, I made my final supper of the trip. As I ate it in silence, I remembered reading how the ancient Hebrews ate their final supper as slaves in Egypt. On the morn, they would become a free people and embark on a journey home. Indeed, this was my Passover meal – my Last Supper – my last meal as a hiker. On the morn, I would leave the woods – and journey home. There was an excitement to the meal – an anticipation – that lent a most splendid taste to the otherwise common dehydrated beef and rice meal.

I ate a relaxing, quiet meal, and was soon overwhelmed with how refreshed I had begun to feel. The tiredness was steadily eroding, and strength once more was flowing through my aching body.

After finishing dinner and clearing the area of remaining food morsels, I turned my attention to the fire. I had already changed into dryer clothing, but had greatly desired to dry my boots out overnight.

As daylight slowly ebbed, I labored over the fire. At times it seemed that I had created a blaze that would burn independent of my worries. But without dry wood to keep it fueled, the flames slowly disappeared. I relit, blew, and fanned, and then repeated the process many times. When I was down to my final two matches I decided to give up the obsession, and simply wait out the coming darkness without a blazing companion.

In the final light of the day I took a quiet stroll around the Shelter area that led me to the forest's edge. I thought perhaps that on the eve of my final night, my contemplative wanderings might inspire some insightful, reflective thought to sum up my thru-hike. Perhaps with so much of the trip behind me, I could formulate some sage thoughts that might be of benefit to the next wanderer. Instead, however, I was seized upon by two ideas that throttled all other thinking. The first was that of a long, hot shower. I played the shower over in my mind until I could nearly feel the steaming, soapy water washing over me. I rehearsed how I would scrub my face and hair. In my mind, I practiced washing the back of my neck, and then my arms and legs. I ran through the whole process and then started it over again. Finally, I envisioned just simply standing in the shower until the water turned cold. I watched a week's worth of grime swill around the drain and disappear. I could hardly wait.

The second thought that plagued my mind was of another luxury: ice cream. I had inherited a fondness – nay, a passion – for ice cream from my dad. Some children learn from their fathers a trade or driving interest. Mine showed me that a day was not truly complete until a generous scoop of vanilla ice cream was dished out and buried beneath heavy chocolate syrup. That tradition had made my life richer over the years, and it was one that I was proud to have received, and honored to pass on. However, I had now gone without that requisite for nearly a week, and was nearly going mad from the tastes that my mind began to recall. From vanilla to chocolate and every colorful flavor in between I let my fantasies go unchecked. Finally, I settled the matter when my mind sampled vanilla ice cream covered with blueberries in heavy syrup. I knew at that moment that nothing short of a blueberry sundae would end my infinite cravings. It was now just a matter of time.

Having ended my evening contemplations, and finished my summary meditations, I tromped gladly back to the shelter.

At last, light faded from the sky and the evening came fully upon the forest. I crawled into my sleeping bag and was amazed as to the sheer darkness of the night. I sorely missed the companionship of the fire. It was a fairly warm summer night, and so I did not fret the cold. Instead, it was the soft light and warm friendliness of the fire that I was missing. Without it, everything seemed damp and dark. Without it, I felt as if the shelter in which I slept was no different than a padded area beneath a tree somewhere in the middle of the woods. Without it, I felt strangely exposed.

The nearby bubbling stream helped orient me, and it provided a break in the otherwise quiet night. Eventually, there in the blackness of the woods my tired mind lost its grip on all awareness, and I fell asleep.

Day six

A terrific boom jolted me from my deep sleep. It was immediately followed by a brilliant flash of light. I sleepily looked up from my pillow and felt a sheet of cold rain blow in through the shelter opening. It was still very much night – probably sometime after midnight – and an electrical storm was rolling through Laurel Mountain.

Remaining in my sleeping bag, I wiggled a little farther back from the shelter opening to keep out of the rain. The continued flashes of lightning were followed by equally impressive roars of thunder. I have always loved a good thunderstorm, and from the front row seat of the shelter floor I was in a perfect position to enjoy the show.

The storm was intense. Each discharge of atmospheric static lit the forest with such intensity that it seemed to be the middle of the day. As if the electricity had touched off a powder keg, the lightning was then followed with a thunderous explosion that rocked the tiny wood frame I slept beneath. I pictured myself lying beneath a lofty battlefield, where the denizens of the sky were engaged in a deadly struggle for this space on Laurel Mountain. I would be the spoil of their raging quarrel.

Playfully I lay breathlessly in my sleeping bag, afraid to make a sound for fear of drawing the attention of these

Thor-like gods. Instinctively my body winced as another crack of thunder shook the night air, and I pushed myself deeper into my bag. As the minutes passed the storm began to relocate. The warriors of the night had not discovered me, and they were moving on – taking their fight with them as they retreated. The hard rain soon began to soften, and the peace of the forest began to return. It was both enjoyable and exhilarating to be so utterly exposed to the violent storm.

As I lay listening to the distant sounds of the storm, my ears pricked up over what seemed to be a different noise. In silence I lay listening until I heard it again. Above the patter of rain it seemed to me that I could hear movement emanating from the woods near the shelter. Something was moving within a few yards of where I lay.

The playful imaginations I had previously entertained were suddenly replaced with some genuine alarm. I strained my ears to reach past the gently falling rain for something that I hoped that I would not discover. I listened quietly and just when I was convinced that I had heard nothing, the noise repeated itself.

It seemed certain that something was moving quietly near the shelter. I listened for other noises – grunts, growls, or the grinding of teeth – but heard nothing. I pined once more over the absence of a campfire, and considered flashing my light through the woods. But I was concerned that the light might illuminate something I did not wish to see, and so I stilled myself and listened.

While listening to the occasional and soft movements of my nocturnal visitor, I was taken back a few years to another night that I had spent in the woods without a campfire. I had been hiking the Appalachian Trail through Maryland, and was spending the night in the deep woods of Michaux State Forest. For reasons now forgotten to me, I had not made a campfire that night. I was alone and sleeping in a small, single-person tent. At around four o'clock in the morning I was awakened by a long shrill scream that sounded from atop the ridge that I was lying beneath. I was not certain what kind of creature made the noise, and, coming out of a deep sleep, was not even sure at first that I had actually heard it. But after a few moments the scream sounded again. This time it was considerably closer. Judging from the sound it seemed that the screamer was moving across the top of the ridge.

I recall trying in vain to disappear. I was sorely frightened by the noise and could not imagine the kind of creature that must have produced it. When the scream was sounded for the third time, it took all of my will not to join in. I could not imagine why a creature would be traveling through the woods at night screaming. I calculated that the animal was prowling around frightening its prey into a state of paralysis and then devouring it. Or worse, I thought, perhaps the screaming animal had just encountered an even more terrifying creature than itself in the woods. That reasoning caused my panic to double. I was so frightened that I was certain my pounding heart was going to draw the creature in to investigate.

I lay awake that night for a long time but never heard the scream again. The remainder of that trip was uneventful, and the night's adventure provided excellent fodder for some great, late-night fireside chats.

As I lay in the Decker Ave Shelters listening to the dying rain, the occasional rustle from outside of the shelter told me that the animal was still present. I dismissed the possibility of a bear since the animal sounded too light-footed. Soon, the noise began to diminish and the intervals between its sounds lengthened. Sleepiness replaced alarm, and my vigilance began to wane.

When my eyes fluttered again, it was just before sunrise. The birds of the early shift were repairing the forest from the previous night's storm, making their presence joyfully known. The sweet fragrance of a dampened forest greeted my nostrils. Another celebration of the daily cycle was already in progress; one that takes place each and every day – whether we are present for it or not.

Normally I would have rolled over and without much effort forced myself back to sleep. But today was different. Today I was going home.

I crawled out of my sleeping bag and rose to my knees. With soiled hands I wiped the sleep from my eyes and scratched my scalp that lay below the stiffly matted rug upon my head. My body tingled with excitement, and instantly I felt fully awake. I decided to forgo breakfast. I had scheduled a morning ride, and felt the need to quickly begin the final leg of my journey.

I fit my bedroll and sleeping bag back into my backpack and gathered whatever belongings had been left out overnight. My boots were still wet from the previous day's rain, but my feet did not object as they took their respective places inside their leather encasements. The air was cool and noticeably damp. Unable to get a weather reading from the sky, I slipped on my rain jacket as a prophylactic measure, and switched my headlamp on. I glanced around the cozy shelter to be certain that I had not left anything behind. Seeing nothing, I turned towards the trail.

I am afraid that I still am unable to comment on the distance between the Laurel Highlands Hiking Trail and the Decker Ave Shelters. Just as my trip off of the trail and into the shelters was prolonged by extreme fatigue, my trip out was fueled by an excitement that seemed to swallow up the steps. Before I knew it, I was standing on the trail. I could not help but smile as I turned my headlamp in a northwardly direction and began following its beckoning beam.

Within a few steps I encountered the sixty-five mile marker post. The sight of it propelled my excitement. I now had only five miles to hike. Gingerly I walked past it, and soon began a small ascent. A noise to my right caught my attention. Looking that way I saw the white tail of a deer bouncing rapidly away from me.

As I reached the summit of the first ascent, I discovered that I did not need my headlamp any longer. The beautiful orange of an early morning summer sky was casting a sufficient and glorious light. I turned off the lamp and removed it from my head. I then crossed over the small summit. From this point it was all downhill – literally. For the next five miles I would descend around 1400 feet off of Laurel Mountain. The trail ends at 1311 feet above sea level – about 90 feet higher than where it begins in Ohiopyle. I had walked this section before, and was looking forward to its casual descent.

Within a few minutes walk, I came across the WJAC TV tower, which is plainly visible from the trail. On the other side of it is an old fire tower. The top of the fire tower is accessed by climbing the zigzagging staircase. But a locked fence at the bottom of the tower keeps curious hikers like me from exploring its view.

As I moved forward, I marveled at the sheer beauty of the forest in the gentle morning light. Everything seemed to exude a soft and quiet glow. It was as though the woods itself had not fully roused from its tranquil slumber. Although the forest never seems hurried, on this particular morning it was as if the hands of the clock were un-busy, folded, and at rest. My passage through the quiet sanctuary was heralded by an increase in song from the avian chorus above, which seemed to sense my early morning delight. Their cantata echoed my mirth and increased my sensation of expectation.

The sights, smells, and sounds produced in the woods in the early morning are like none other. It is a special hour. It is as though the trees themselves are rested and relaxed, casting only the shadow of gentle care across a peaceful floor. Although my feet felt like running and dancing this morning, out of respect for the noiseless forest, I let them fall subdued along the path. But inwardly I felt a great joy. I felt excitement.

It seemed I had only been walking a few moments when I reached the sixty-six mile marker; four miles to go. At this point the trail begins to take a northeasterly course, seeking the edge of the Conemaugh Gorge. Before long I began hearing the occasional sounds of traffic from Route 56 as early morning commuters were journeying toward their own destinations.

The path soon found the rim of the Conemaugh Gorge. This is a deep ravine cutting off the northern edges of Laurel Hill and Chestnut Ridge. At the bottom of the gorge courses the Conemaugh River. The river begins in the heart of Johnstown, Pennsylvania, where the Little Conemaugh and Stoneycreek Rivers join together. It then flows approximately seventy miles in a northwesterly direction, ending in Saltsburg, Pennsylvania. There it joins Loyalhanna Creek to become the Kiskiminetas – or The Kiski River. The Kiski River flows to Freeport, Pennsylvania, where it joins the Allegheny River, and after a short trip helps form the Ohio River. Ultimately, the Youghiogheny River waters encountered at the beginning of the Laurel Highlands trail, and the Conemaugh River waters at its end will share the same destination.

From certain vantage points along the edge of the ravine, one can sometimes catch stunning glimpses of the gorge. In the springtime the view is uninhibited by the foliage allowing a much wider view of the valley. But in the autumn, when the colors reach their peak, if one can find one of the rocky perches along the edge, the view is simply breathtaking.

As I walked along the edge of the valley this summer day, portions of the Conemaugh Gorge were glimpsed through the heavy leaves. Heavy fog, like a fluffy cotton blanket, covered the floor of the valley below me, giving it a pure, but mysterious appearance. Out of the fog, I heard the unmistakable roar of a locomotive as it churned alongside the roadway on its iron trail.

Just past mile marker sixty-seven, I stopped to remove my rain jacket. The sky was as clear as could be hoped for. There was no leftover hint of the early morning's storm, or a shadow of impending rain. The air was still cool, but very comfortable for walking.

As I was tying my jacket to my backpack, my eye caught a strange rock formation just west of the trail. I had not recalled seeing the formation before, and so I was inspired to investigate. The rocks were set upon each other to form what appeared to be an old foundation. Two of its corners were still evident, appearing about fifteen feet wide. I could not determine if the structure had been square or rectangular, and therefore could not estimate its original size. I could not find any evidence of the building that had likely been raised upon the foundation. Most probable it had been torn down, with only the stones left as a reminder of its existence. During the middle to late 1800s a stone quarry operated from this side of the mountain, and it seemed possible to me that this structure had once belonged to that operation.

Continuing northward, I passed the sixty-eight mile post and heard what sounded like the sizzling of bacon frying in a pan. Drawing closer to the source, I saw towering power lines in a swath cut through the forest. The crackling sound came from the heavy electrical lines that were carrying its charged cargo from the nearby Conemaugh Power Station. As I stepped out into the narrow opening, I looked to the west and saw smoke belching from the plant's stacks. To the east the view of the gorge is somewhat marred by the power lines creeping up the adjacent hillside. I did not linger long, but crossed the opening and continued my descent.

As I continued down the footpath, I came across one of the most unusual sites along the trail: a rusted, candy cane-shaped metal pipe extending from a huge boulder. Like the fabled Sword in the Stone, the pipe is solidly embedded in the rock waiting for a hiker more worthy than I to remove it. But being more than just an oddity to gaze at, the pipe is a waypoint for an interesting find.

Since I was well ahead of schedule, I decided to take the time to explore this relatively unknown piece of history that the trail offers. From the pipe, I turned around and began to walk south for about fifty yards. By keeping a lookout to the left, there appears a break in the stone wall. I passed through the break, and down a short, steep descent. At the bottom of the descent appears a passageway of sorts, almost completely covered by rhododendron. I crawled through the portal and set my backpack down. I knew the climb back out would be too steep for the extra weight. I then began to descend the remains of an old quarry incline.

Down the incline, I carefully climbed until I reached the bottom. There, covered with moss and leaves, with a few young trees growing over its top, is the old quarry platform. Made of huge, hand-cut stone blocks, the platform seems to have once been a loading dock for stone that was harvested from the mountain side. The quarry has been out of operation since around 1930 and now rests inaudibly in the woods.

It's a beautiful, quiet place. High above the platform is a solid rock wall that conceals the platform from the trail. Added to this is thick, leafy Mountain Laurel that extends out from the rocks to help shield the lonely place. The forest near the platform is young and not as dense as in other places. Therefore, from the quarry dock one has a great vantage point overlooking the hillside.

I sat down upon one of the stone blocks and tried to imagine the quarry work that would have been taking place a century before. I pictured men and their companion beasts of burden working to extract the heavy sandstone from the mountain. These would then have been cut to predetermined size with simple tools. Staring at the incline, one can almost see the solid rock being brought down the steep hillside to the platform. From there it would be shipped to waiting destinations to construct homes, factories, churches, or whatever building that its architects were designing to stand the test of time.

I listened for the clank of tools, the pounding of hammers, and the braying of animals. I watched for tired men ending their shifts, and for refreshed ones replacing them. I sniffed the air for the persistent musk of sandstone dust, mixed with human sweat. And I felt the rocky texture of stone being ground against callused skin as they were moved with tired muscles.

It is said that stone from this quarry was cut and delivered to Johnstown where it was used to build the still-standing stone bridge located near present-day Point Stadium. In 1889, that bridge became famous when Johnstown was devastated by a brutal flood. It began when the South Fork Dam gave way and a wall of water reaching as high as sixty feet roared down on the unsuspecting city.

Every bridge in town was washed away by the watery visitation – except for the stone bridge. At its arches, a thirty-acre debris field of material, animals, and living and dead souls gathered. While efforts were being made to rescue those trapped at the bridge, the debris field caught fire. It burned for days bringing a horrific demise to many of its victims.

After completing my visit to the quarry platform, I began the very difficult ascent up the incline to the trail. I had to stop many times to catch my breath and was infinitely glad that I had not brought my backpack down the hill. When I hitched myself to it again, I crawled through the rhododendron opening and returned to the trail. I passed once more the muted, candy caned-shaped pipe, and continued my journey northward.

The trail was especially kind today, and was descending at an inviting pace. I followed it through the twists and turns as it slid me closer along to my objective. Finally, I came to the sixty-nine mile post. I nearly cheered. Smiling broadly I passed it and began my final mile.

Solo hiking the Laurel Highlands Hiking Trail – like any trail – is more than just a physical test of endurance. It is a mental and emotional challenge as well. Making camp at night is always easier when there are more hands available to carry firewood. As well, there are moments of boredom, when one yearns for the company of others. There are times when one stands before a magnificent or unusual scene and recognizes the feeling of frustration for not being able to share it. These occasions are absorbed by the hiker who chooses to walk in the woods alone, with the hope of a reward that will outweigh its disappointments.

At the bottom of the mountain the trail crosses a logging road. Plainly visible to the west of this is the Big Springs Reservoir. It is a small body of water that helps hydrate nearby Seward. I had explored its shores a few times before, and decided today I would continue past it.

As I moved on ahead, the path became wider and even easier to walk. I bounced effortlessly along, wandering in innocent pleasure. Then, quite unexpectedly I saw it. My mind had been elsewhere occupied, and so I was not even thinking about it. Yet, there it stood: the seventy-mile marker. My walk was over.

I stopped at the marker and reached out to touch it. It was course to the touch, and though it had been symmetrical at one time, was now quite misshapen. I loosened my backpack and put both poles into my right hand. Dropping to one knee, I offered a prayer of thanksgiving and praise. No one could have pried the smile from my lips. I felt full. I felt satisfied. I felt completed.

Just beyond the last marker was the parking lot. I walked to it and removed my backpack. Suddenly, I felt a bit disoriented. Not in the sense of being lost, but as if I did not know what to do next. For the past six days I had only one thing to do: walk. Now that that objective had been removed I was not sure what to do with myself.

As I lingered in the parking lot, near the trail entrance, a green minivan pulled into a parking space. I watched a young man get out and walk to the side door. He slid it open and bent inside of the vehicle. I could see that he was gathering together some equipment. He then removed his tennis shoes from his feet and withdrew some well-worn hiking boots from the van. With care, he firmly laced each one up, and then pulled from the vehicle a light gray and blue backpack. He attached it to his back and picked out some final items from the vehicle that he stuffed into his pockets. Then, locking the doors of the vehicle and attaching the keys to his belt he turned and walked towards me.

"Looks like you're going to have a great day for hike!" I called out as he drew closer.

"Ah, it's gonna be a great day." He replied with a smile that was just as deep as it was broad. "What about you? Are you coming or going?" he asked as he paused near the trail.

"Just finished up this morning," I replied as I slowly stood up and brushed myself off. I could hear the satisfaction in my own voice.

"You must have had an early start. Where did you come in from?" he continued.

"I left from Decker Ave just a few hours ago." I sensed a flavor in my voice that I had never heard before.

"How long have you been out?" My new friend asked with excitement in his voice.

"Today is day six. I began in Ohiopyle, and just completed the trail a few minutes before you pulled up." The tone in my voice was there again. I did not know what it represented, but I liked it.

"Oh, that's great!" he said with what sounded like genuine excitement. "I'm starting today, and hope to be in Ohiopyle in about the same amount of time that it took you! I've hiked some sections of the trail before, and have always wanted to do an end-to-end hike; just never got around to it – until today."

There was real animation in his voice. His eyes sparkled with enthusiasm, and his face revealed an eager spirit.

"Did you have a good time?" he asked.

I paused at his question. I knew the answer but I wanted to mull it over for just a moment. The Laurel Highlands Hiking Trail had offered some challenging terrain, and on some of its hillsides I stood really questioning why I was there. But with the muscle aches now soothed, the chaffed skin no longer being rubbed, and breathing finally unlabored, I could look back with a clear mind and give him a convincing answer.

"I loved it." I said with a smile.

"Cool" he responded. "Well, I gotta get going." He said as he started to turn towards the trail.

"Good luck!" I called. "I hope that you have a great time as well."

As he turned from me I had a late thought. "Hold on a second," I said.

He paused and turned around, still bearing his friendly smile. I dug around in my pocket not even sure if it was still there. But finally my fingers felt its smooth edges, and I pulled out the small colorful pebble that I had picked up on my first day. I looked it over for a second and then tossed it to him. He caught it with an unspoken question on his face.

"I picked that up in Ohiopyle. Could you carry it back for me?" I asked matching his smile with mine.

"I'd love to," he replied without missing a beat.

My friend pulled a red kerchief out of one of his pockets and carefully wrapped the pebble inside. He then stuffed it into a side pocket of his hiking pants and zippered it closed. He gave me a wave that showed me he knew what he was to do, and I returned his fraternal salute. He then disappeared into the woods to seek out his own adventure while I returned to a seated position against my backpack.

I waited in the parking lot for at least another hour before my parents arrived. I then loaded my gear into the back of their van and we pulled away. They caught me up on news and family events, and had many questions. At times, however, the conversation fell silent. It was then that I would look out of the window at the trees and mountain rolling past. I could not deny the strong longing to return and walk some more.

Epilogue

It has been years now since I finished the walk across Laurel Mountain. The leaky boots that disappointed my feet were exchanged for a sturdier, more faithful pair. I introduced them quickly to the trail and together we have made many visits. Thankfully, they have acquired a particular fondness for walking. Even now, they wait patiently by my door for another invitation.

As I write these words, it is a tremendously autumn day. The colors of fall are sprinkling the landscape in a final display of beauty before the drab gray of winter settles in. The wind is still warm though, and as it blows across my front porch where I sit, I catch a hint of evergreen. The smell is enchanting. My feet begin to feel restless; my boots grow impatient; there is much walking yet to do.

Made in the USA
Lexington, KY
28 November 2019